HOW TO MANAGE (HELPMEET) A MILLION DOLLAR MAN
WAITING ON MY RUTH EXPERIENCE REVISED

LATRICIA TAYLOR

JESUS KINGDOM LIFE MINISTRY SELF PUBLISHING CO.

Copyright © 2020 by Latricia Taylor

All rights reserved.

No part of this book may be reproduced in any form or by any electronic or mechanical means, including information storage and retrieval systems, without written permission from the author, except for the use of brief quotations in a book review.

Scripture taken from the HOLY BIBLE, NEW INTERNATIONAL VERSION ®. NIV®. COPYRIGHT © 1973, 1978, 1984, 2011 by Biblica, Inc.®. Used by permission. All rights reserved worldwide.

Edited by Evangelist Kimberly Hicks email: kimberly1259@yahoo.com

I want to dedicate this book in loving memory of my mother, Mary Nelson RIH 1939 to 2009. She is the strongest woman I know. She is and will always be my inspiration.

To my children, you guys have been my motivation to live my reasons for pushing forward and not giving up: my biological sister's niece and nephew. Also, my sisters in Christ past and present (JKLM) that has been a role model and influential in helping me to grow into the woman I am today thank you for your love and support. And last but not least, Melvin Marks, who was heaven-sent, I'm eternally grateful for his spiritual guidance and direction I know he has received his crown RIH.

Above all, I'm most grateful to my Lord and Savior, Jesus Christ, who makes all things possible!

CONTENTS

Introduction vii

Chapter 1   1
Chapter 2   9
Chapter 3   18
Chapter 4   34
Chapter 5   44
Chapter 6   60
Chapter 7   77
Chapter 8   94
Chapter 9   104
Chapter 10   115
Chapter 11   131
Chapter 12   141
Chapter 13   149
Chapter 14   167

About the Author   175

INTRODUCTION

A MAN OF GODLY CHARACTER IS HARD TO FIND

"The number one priority of humanity is material security."

-Dr. Miles Monroe

The question that many of us struggle within the Kingdom of God. What God's will is; His plans, and His purpose for our lives. I have been asked this question many times in different settings with other believers. What is it that I desire from God? One time in a women's group, this question came up, and the person that was leading the discussion asked each of us individually what we desire from the Lord. Most of the women's answers were: "a good husband, a great job." The majority of their feedback was materialistic and self-motivated. Subsequently, that's what most people are motivated by materialism. I listened to them without making any judgments. However, when it was my turn, my answer shocked them: "I want to be in God's will." When I said that the room got quiet and the person that was leading the conversation asked me again like I didn't understand what she said the first time. I answered her earnestly, "I want to be in God's will." Based on their reaction, they didn't believe that I was sincere. I didn't say that just to be saying something profound, I truly meant it!

INTRODUCTION

They didn't know me or what I had been through when I came to Christ, and I was exhausted with this world and people, I needed God to rescue me. I had material things; they didn't bring me any fulfillment. Those things didn't keep me happy. I needed something that material things and people couldn't give me: PURPOSE! One of my favorite scriptures that speaks to my heart:

Psalms 27:4 KJV

"One thing have I desired of the Lord, that will I seek after; that I may dwell in the house of the Lord all the days of my life, to behold the beauty of the Lord, and to enquire in His temple."

Today, I can genuinely say, I found my purpose in God! A few years prior, I was an owner and operator of a hair salon in Flint, MI. One day the clients, stylists, and I was having a conversation about our future. Mind you at this time; I wasn't attending church. I remember one of the ladies saying she wanted to be an Airline Stewardess. They all had high goals and money-making ventures that they wanted to accomplish. I anxiously burst out and said, "I want to be in God's will." At that time, I didn't understand what that meant to be in God's will. I believe God was confirming His plans for my future. I still feel the same way today; I just want to be in God's will. The word will, in Greek means "God's desire." If you delight yourself in Him, not your intention, He will give you the desires of your heart.

(See Psalms 37:34)

Matthew 6:33 KJV

"But seek ye first the Kingdom of God, and His righteousness and all these things shall be added unto you."

Our motivation for seeking God shouldn't be for material gain and personal satisfaction; that's the behavior of the world, religion, and unbelievers. (*See Matthew 6:31-32*) However, our motivation should be to be in an intimate relationship, love, and citizenship with God. His Kingdom has all the financial, emotional, and personal security we will ever need. When you align yourself with His Kingdom structure, we have access to His benefits. Like any government, there are rules, laws, and regulations, and the same applies to God's Kingdom.

Kingdom First:

What does God desire?

Matthew 6:10 KJV

That His Kingdom come, Thy will be done in earth, as it is in heaven."

"God desires earth to be like it is in heaven, in obedience to His rule, laws, and regulations."

What is God's Plan?

Jeremiah 29:11 NIV

"For I know the plans I have for you, declares the Lord, plans to prosper you and not to harm you, plans to give you hope and a future."

Focus a moment on the words I and know. I mean, God is referring to Himself. Know means knowing. In other words, God is saying I have the knowledge of my will, my plans, and my purpose for your lives. Not our mothers, nor our fathers have this information unless God reveals it to them. They were simply the vehicles God used to get us here for His divine purpose. Jeremiah 1:5 gives us confirmation of the predestined plan and purpose of God for humankind through Jeremiah, His prophet.

Jeremiah 1:5 NIV

"Before I formed you in the womb, I knew you, before you were born; I set you apart; I appointed you as a prophet to the nations."

What God is saying to Jeremiah is what He is saying to us, our very existence here on earth, He knew of, He had planned for, and it is for His divine purpose.

INTRODUCTION

"God's plans are for us to be socially and economically prosperous. Not at the expense of us spiritually debilitated."

What is God's purpose?

We all have a purpose as to why we were born. The greatest fulfillment is to know what it is. God's mission is to fulfill whatever He has proposed for each one of us, the earth, His Kingdom, and His Word. Our purpose is to find out what it is.

Psalms 57:2 NIV

"I cry out to God Most High, to God, who fulfills His purpose for me."

Isaiah 46:10-11 NIV

"I make known the end from the beginning, from ancient times, what is still to come. I say, My purpose will stand, and I will do all that I please. From the east, I summon a bird of prey; from a far-off land, a man to fulfill my purpose. What I have said that I will bring about; what I have planned, that I will do." (See also Romans 8:28.)

In movies, screenplays and literature, there are some basic character types. The hero: "protagonist" and the opposite being an "antagonist." Every story has these types of characters, and the story revolves around them. The word "protagonist" means being an advocate or champion of a cause or idea. The term "antagonist" means a person who actively opposes or is hostile to someone or something, an adversary. Not only is this concept used in literature, but it's also a depiction of how the world is. It's a description of humanity. We live in a protagonist, and antagonist existence and life revolve around it. Our advocate (protagonist) is Jesus, our adversary (antagonist) is Satan. Another way to look at it is our Savior (protagonist), opposes the thief (antagonist). Inhumanity, the protagonist and antagonist are our struggles within us with both good and evil. Unfortunately, the adversary has a plan as well.

INTRODUCTION

John 10:10 NKJV

"The thief does not come except to steal, and to kill, and to destroy. I have come that they may have life and that they may have it more abundantly."

1 Peter 5:8 NIV

"Be alert and sober mind. Your enemy, the devil, prowls around like a roaring lion looking for someone to devour."

However, in scriptwriting and any literature, the author has the authority. They control characters, the plot, scheme, scene description, location, victories, defeats, beginning, middle, and the end of the story. In this exposition called life, God (Jesus) is the author, and He has overcome the devil on our behalf. In His Book, He has given us the authority through Him, the protagonist (hero) to overcome and counteract any plans, plots, schemes, hurts, and pains that have inflicted on us, or that intended to cause harm by the enemy. Jesus is our hero His Book is a best seller!

Overcome Your Past

Revelation 12:11 KJV

"And they overcame him by the blood of the Lamb and by the word of our testimony, and they loved not their lives unto death."

He has written down all the tools we need to be victorious in the Bible. No matter what has happened to you in the past, you are an overcomer. Because you've lived to tell it, other women have experienced the same thing or worse than what you have been through and didn't survive. Because you survived, that is an indication that you have a purpose. The author didn't write you out. You can't move forward if you are stuck in your past. Don't be your antagonist. If you haven't forgiven, forgive; move forward into this new experience. The author has written it, and it shall come to pass. As the writer in

INTRODUCTION

Hebrews says: fix your eyes on Him, the author and the finisher of your faith.

Hebrew 12:1-2 NIV

"Therefore, since we are surrounded by such a great cloud of witnesses, let us throw off everything that hinders and the sin that so easily entangles. And let us run with perseverance the race marked out for us, fixing our eyes on Jesus, the pioneer, and perfecter of faith. For the joy set before him, he endured the cross, scorning its shame, and sat down at the right hand of the throne of God."

"Our very existence here on earth He knew of, He had planned for, and it is for His divine purpose."

CHAPTER 1

WOUNDED WITH PURPOSE: THE BOOK OF RUTH

*E*very woman wants to find their true love. Most Kingdom women read the Book of Ruth in hopes of finding their own 21st century Boaz. The Book of Ruth is not just a love story; it reveals the beauty of loyalty, servitude, devotion, and selfless purpose. Why is the Book of Ruth an essential book in the Bible? Primarily because it's relevant to the events leading up to the birth, earthly ministry, death, burial, and resurrection, of our Lord and Savior Jesus Christ. It's a book of principles, purpose, and the establishment of His Kingdom. The Old Testament contains signs, symbols, and examples of what is to come. So, every event, person, and their relationships have significant meaning and purpose. Even when it comes to our relationships, God desires them to serve a legitimate role. When God created Adam and Eve, He created them to fulfill a purpose.

Genesis NIV 1:28

"God blessed them and said to them, be fruitful and increase in number; fill the earth, and subdue it. Rule over the fish in the sea and the birds in the sky and over every living creature that moves on the ground."

Meaningless relationships are nonproductive. God created relationships to be productive; we are not here just to take up space. Just as love is essential, productivity is vital as well. We are here to supply a need, produce, and reproduce I know some are self-centered. Self-centered people believe the world revolves around them. Truthfully, it's not about us, it's about purpose, just as it wasn't about the three women who are the focal point of the message found in the Book of Ruth; Naomi, Ruth, and Orpah. I was listening to a broadcast on Periscope where this young man was speaking about the Book of Ruth. He was saying (sarcastically) women are still looking for their Boaz. He told the women to stop looking for Boaz, Boaz is dead. Boaz may be gone; however, the concept, characteristics/attributes, and principles of his character are yet noble and desirable, that hasn't changed. If you apply the same principles, you will get the same or similar results. *Meaningless relationships are a waste of time. Your time is valuable.*

Naomi

Naomi was married with two sons, and they initially resided in Bethlehem Judah. Because of famine in Bethlehem Judah, Naomi's family migrated to a place called Moab. Unfortunately, during their stay, her husband died, which left her a widow. After the passing of her husband, Naomi remained in Moab for ten years. Within those ten years, her sons met Ruth and Orpah, and they married these two Moabite women. Naomi suffered two other unfortunate, tragic events, the death of both of her sons. The Bible says Naomi were left without her two sons and her husband. The word left means to go away from, to abandon. Naomi felt abandoned. (*Ruth chapter 1*)

In the midst of this, Naomi decided to leave Moab after the death of her sons. Subsequently, as you see, her husband's death didn't motivate her to move. It wasn't until her sons died, and she heard of the Lord's provision in Bethlehem Judah that she felt the urge to leave Moab. The lack of Judah motivated them to go; God's provision motivated her to return home. The reality was she couldn't go until she fulfilled her purpose in Moab. However, she didn't leave alone. She and her two daughters-in-law (which had a purpose) headed back home with her. She suffered a significant loss in Moab. I believe she felt there was nothing else left for her there but bad memories. The only relatives she had died. She left the place where she became wounded, but in the process of her departure, note that it was a physical relocation, not a mental one. She was devastated by her tragedies, and as a result, the Bible says she changed her name. How many of us have been and are presently wounded? You've left the situation, place, and the people physically, however, you are still carrying them mentally? I carried a wound for years from losing my business, home, so-called friends, and events that had happened in my relationships that led to divorce. Like Naomi, the only thing that was holding me in Flint, Michigan, was my mother. After my mother passed away, the Lord allowed me to relocate. I left Flint, but I took the wounds from Flint with me. Some people believe their life will change for the better if they could leave the place where it all happened. However, we must remember wherever we go; we are taking us with us.

Another perspective on relocation; God will take you away from people and places so that He can love you back to health and wholeness. To make a long story short, after my move, some years had passed, and I attended a service. The minister called me out and began to prophesy to me. She said the Lord was taking me through a transition, and I fell out on the floor. Transition means the process or a period of changing from one state or condition to another. When I got up; I had a bitter taste in my mouth. I went home. I still had that bitter taste in my mouth. I told my friend who was visiting me at the time. She explained to me by the leading of the Holy Spirit that the Lord used the bitter taste to expose the condition of my heart. I was indeed angry. I didn't and couldn't deny it, because it was true. I looked up the word bitter for clarity. Some attributes of bitterness are; anger, hurt, or resentfulness because of one's lousy experience or sense of unjust treatment. Yes, that was me. Just like Naomi, she became bitter.

Ruth 1:20 NIV

"Don't call me Naomi, she told them. Call me Mara, because The Almighty has made me bitter."

Pay attention to what she said in the latter portion of the scripture. The Lord Almighty has made me bitter. In other words, she was blaming God. There are many people angry at God but just won't admit it even though many of the things that have happened in our lives were because of man's or woman's own will. I believe He understands and can relate because He's familiar with tragedies and loss. God lost (gave) His son (Jesus Christ) to the purpose.

Isaiah 53:3 NIV

"He was despised and rejected by mankind, a man of suffering, and familiar with pain. Like one from whom people hide their faces He was despised, and we held Him in low esteem."

Our purpose has a cost, and we may suffer loss. There may be some painful experiences we may have to endure. However, your mission is more significant than your pain. We discussed earlier; it's not about us. I believe He is a loving God; He gives us time alone with Him to help us grieve healthily. The name Naomi means "pleasantness." In the Old Testament, the names often were given to describe the character of the individual. Pleasantness was her former state before her loss. How many of us have changed our official name and became the names of our situation? Depression, suicide, bitterness, oppression, suppression, etc., *the pain has a purpose; just don't let it define your life.*

PRINCIPLE OF CONFESSION

Every Kingdom has laws; principles are rules or beliefs governing one's behavior. God's principles establish the lifestyle in His Kingdom, the word governing means to control or have influence over one's actions and emotions. God honors His principles. It was said God's laws do not change. God is the same yesterday, today and forever. Naomi demonstrated a principle. The principle of confession

1 John 1:9 KJV

"If we confess our sins, he is faithful and just to forgive us our sins and to cleanse us from all unrighteousness."

When you suppress your feelings, it produces unforgiveness. God created everything to reproduce after its kind. Characteristics bring forth other components; for example, Naomi is bitter, bitterness builds anger and resentment these attributes if you fester them, they will create unforgiveness. Confession produces healing, restoration, and forgiveness. Also, it releases and dismisses the power and the influence of the enemy. The word confession is: "homologeo homolog-eh," in Greek the term means to say the same, agree, admit, and acknowledge. The context must determine delineated nature. It can mean to recognize sin or to acknowledge someone or something.

James 5:16 NIV

"Therefore, confess your sins one to each other and pray for each other so that you may be healed. The prayer of a righteous person is powerful and effective."

Righteousness is another principle within the Kingdom; in fact, it is the governing principle of all other policies produced by Matthew 6:33. Matthew 5:6. James says the power and results come through the prayers of the righteous. Remember earlier; I said if you apply His principles, you will get results. The original Greek word righteous is "dikaios," which means those who are upright, just, conforming to God's laws. A related term, "dikaiosune," means righteousness or uprightness.

Romans 3:22 NIV

"This righteousness is given through faith in Jesus Christ to all who believe. There is no difference between Jew and Gentile,"

Because a person has qualifications by title doesn't mean they are qualified. Look for these qualities in a person so you can avoid what some have suffered, known as "church hurt." Seek out someone who will protect your confidentiality. Therefore, because Naomi confessed her truth, she was able to receive healing and restoration, which we will talk about later. However, it didn't happen immediately, but she was in the process.

John 8:32 NIV

"Then you will know the truth, and the truth will set you free."

QUALITIES OF RIGHTEOUSNESS:

- Moral Uprightness

- Faith

- Believer

Principles of Confession:

- Acknowledgment

- Forgiveness

"CONFESSION PREVENTS a person from having unhealthy relationships. With confession, your truth makes you free."

WHAT MEANEST THIS

Ecclesiastes 3:1 KJV

"To everything, there is a season and a time to every purpose under the heaven:"

I had a mentor named Mr. Melvin Marks. He was a wise, spiritual Godly man. We would walk 7 to 9 hours a day praying and ministering the Word of God. It didn't matter if it rained, he would come with a rain jacket and a banana. He passed away a couple of years ago. Although before I left Flint, he told me I was going to leave, he began to prepare me. During the duration of our relationship, God used him. He poured a lot of wisdom into me, and I know he left here empty. Melvin Marks was the most dedicated man I have ever met personally. One of the things he told me was a mans greatest attribute is sensitivity. He also told me that people are in your life to build you up (edify) or tear you down. When you meet people, ask God what meanest this? Be led by the spirit and He will reveal to you what purpose they have in your life. Jesus had twelve disciples. One of them was a devil. The Bible says (*See: John 6:43.*) The devil had a purpose, too; you know the story, betraying Jesus so that Jesus could fulfill His purpose. Jesus had the upper hand because He knew who he was. Jesus was always ahead of the enemy. The Bible also tells us to know who you labor among (*See: 1 Thessalonians 5:12.*) Some relationships are seasonal, and some are for a lifetime. In doing this, it will save you a lot of wasted time, disappointments, heartaches, back-sets, and pain. My mentor, I miss him dearly; he knew his purpose in my life, and he fulfilled it. We remained in touch for a while when I left; then I lost contact because my carrying season was over it was time for me to walk. Naomi didn't go alone; she took the two ladies with her. Separation is not only experienced through death, but departure can also come by way of purpose. Everyone's goal is not to go with us, even those that we love. Once the validity/purpose of their relationship is determined, don't overstay your season. Three things can happen you will be forced to leave on bad terms, you can hinder their purpose, or they can be a hindrance to yours.

"KNOWING your bond with some people may be seasonal, and being aware of what that season is for, can save you unnecessary heartache and pain."

. . .

LATRICIA TAYLOR

"WHAT YOU DON'T KNOW CAN HURT you."

"THEY COME to either build up or to tear down."

CHAPTER 2

HINDERING YOUR PURPOSE: SOME INFORMATION IS SEASONAL; SOME IS FOR A LIFETIME.

It can be detrimental to your purpose if you receive the wrong information or advice at the wrong time. Or it could be the right information at the wrong time, which also makes it incorrect. Besides, be mindful of the source you receive your information. Make sure it's a reliable source. Reliable, not by man's intellect, but by God's Spirit. People can lead you down the wrong path, a path that God didn't intend for you. As was said earlier, people are in our lives for a season or a lifetime. The same applies to information or advice; it can be for a season or a lifetime. However, God will place some influential people in our lives to impart, guide, and instruct us in our purpose. Judging them by social or financial status, their looks, or education, we can miss God. As with me, God used a 6-foot, muscle-bound man with short-shorts to mentor me. He may not have looked the part by society's standards, but he was indeed a Godsend! Though Mr. Marks was knowledgeable, a man full of the Holy Spirit, sent by God, I confirmed it with God. Moreover, he would encourage it. Many factors can distort our judgment.

One, carnality: the meaning of the flesh

Romans 8:7 KJV

"Because the carnal mind is enmity against God: for it is not subject to the law of God, neither indeed can be."

Flesh and spirit, good and evil, is the battle we all face. Apostle Paul explains this as the battle of our members as believers.

Romans 7:21-25 KJV

"I find then a law, that, when I would do good, evil is present with me. For I delight in the law of God after the inward man: But I see another law in my members, warring against the law of my mind, and bringing me into captivity to the law of sin which is my members. O wretched man that I am! who shall deliver me from the body of this death? I thank God through Jesus Christ, our Lord. So then with the mind, I myself serve the law of God, but with the flesh the law of sin."

In 1 John, John, in his universal message, says do not believe every spirit. We must test the spirit to identify whether it's from God because many false prophets have gone into the world (*See: 1 John 4:1-6.*) This passage applies to preachers, teachers, evangelists, apostles, bishops, priests, etc., I'm not saying everyone has bad intentions or even intends to guide you wrong. However, some things have more to do with timing and the seasons of life. I learned this one thing a long time ago from numerous disappointments. Every message is not for me. Everyone is not purposed to speak into my life. For example, on Sunday mornings, the pastor would preach an excellent, encouraging sermon to the congregation. Affirming things, such as you are coming out of your situation, someone's getting ready to bless you this week, the check is in the mail, and it's your season. At the moment, I'm shouting, declaring, decreeing, and receiving it all in the Name of Jesus. However, I didn't see any immediate changes in my situation or my circumstances; in fact, it got worse. As a result, I would be disappointed, frustrated, and above all, question my faith.

My desire was for it to end, so the presentation/sermon sounded good to me. Yet, the reality was the message wasn't for me. I wasn't in a season of restoration—those words catered to my flesh, not my purpose. Don't get me wrong it was for somebody, just not me at that time. At the time, I was in a season where God was stripping me, which wasn't an overnight or even a one-year process. I'm saying all this to say. Some things we can't avoid because it's necessary for your purpose. At the same time, knowing the season you're in, one can prevent somethings. As I said earlier, I cried out to God, and He said: "Every message is not for you." Once He gave me the understanding, I received peace. You heard the phrase, "Eat the meat and spit out the bones."

Ecclesiastes 3:6 KJV

"A time to get and a time to lose; a time to keep, and a time to cast away;"

Two, Personal Bias: A tendency to lean in a specific direction often to the detriment of an open mind. An inclination toward one way of thinking. You must know when to trust the source that was at one time, trustworthy. For example:

Matthew 16:13-17 KJV

"When Jesus came into the coasts of Caesarea Philippi, He asked His disciples, saying, Whom do men say that I the Son of man am? And they said Some say that thou art John the Baptist: some Elias; and others, Jeremias, or one of the prophets. He saith unto them, But whom say ye that I am? And Simon Peter answered and said, Thou art the Christ, the Son of the living God. And Jesus answered and said unto him Blessed art thou, Simon Barjona: for flesh and blood hath not revealed it unto thee, but my Father which is in heaven."

Peter received praise from Jesus because the information he gave Him was accurate. Why was Peter accurate? Because what he heard came from the influence of God.

On another occasion, in the same chapter, Matthew 16:21, Jesus began to talk to His disciples about the things He was going to suffer in Jerusalem. He told them He must die on the third day rise again.

Matthew 16:23 NIV

"Jesus turned and said to Peter, "Get behind me, Satan! You are a stumbling block to me; you do not have in mind the concerns of God, but merely human concerns."

Peter was presumptuous. He received a rebuke from Jesus. Again, Jesus called out another spirit that was influencing Peter, Satan! Peter's flesh! Apostle Paul says with the law of my mind, I serve God but with my flesh the law of sin *Romans 7:25*. I want you to recognize how the same person that produces good can also create evil. The same person that gives you sound advice can also be unreliable at times. Remember, Satan (the thief) has a purpose as well to steal, kill, and destroy (See: John 10:10.) He will use anyone he can to accomplish his mission. Especially those that are the closest to you. Peter was the best candidate to be used as a stumbling block to Jesus's purpose for just that reason; his closeness to Jesus. What impaired Peter, as was defined, his personal bias, the love he had for Jesus.

Moreover, he didn't want Him to suffer. Imagine if it were you and someone you loved told you they were going to endure to the point of death. Would you be biased? To be honest, I don't know what I would do. My first thought probably would be my flesh, to try to talk them out of it. It doesn't matter how anointed and convincing a person is. They still have imperfections. Biased or partial behavior can be a stumbling block to our purpose and compromise our spirituality. Also, ask God for wisdom when you pray for God to remove your stumbling blocks. It may be a loved one; i.e., *husband, children, dear friends, etc.,* allow God's will to prevail over everyone and everything. Pray that you recognize your stumbling blocks so that they will not be a hindrance to your purpose. *Don't allow anyone to talk you out of your mission.*

Orpah

We don't hear much about Orpah in the Bible. The only mention of her is in Ruth, Chapter 1. I'm not saying she wasn't necessary; however, her presence wasn't significant to the main character's purpose: Jesus Christ. Or could it have been? She had the same opportunities as the other ladies. She as well suffered the loss of her husband, Naomi's Son Kilion. She left the place where they lived, to go with Naomi to Bethlehem Judah Ruth 1:7. However, Naomi presented her with another option to go back to her homeland. Perhaps, that didn't cross her mind until Naomi mentioned it.

Ruth 1:8-10 NIV

"Then Naomi said to her two daughters-in-law, "Go back, each of you, to your mother's home. May the Lord show you kindness, as you have shown to your dead and me. May the Lord grant that each of you rest in the home of another husband." Then she kissed them goodbye and they wept aloud and said to her, we will go back with you to your people."

With everything else to consider, she gave her all of the negative reasons why she shouldn't come with her.

Ruth 1:11-13 NIV

"But Naomi said, Return home, my daughters. Why would you come with me? Am I going to have any more sons, who could become your husbands? Return home, my daughters; I am too old to have another husband. Even if I thought there was still hope for me even if I had a husband tonight and then gave birth to sons-- would you wait until they grew up? Would you remain unmarried for them? No, my daughters. It is more bitter for me than for you, because the Lord's hand has turned against me!"

Which brings us to the third reason, our judgment can potentially become distorted.

Third Offense: Offense is defined as having anger, annoyance, or resentment. We read earlier Naomi was bitter, hurt people hurt other people. We can't encourage anyone if we are not supported. We can't give joy if we don't have pleasure. We can't make anyone happy if we are not satisfied. We can only give what we have within us. Some people's advice is centered around their offenses and convictions. It controls their entire thought process. Their conversations are self-centered. They will lead you to believe they're talking about your situation, and they are talking about themselves. With Naomi's current attitude, she shouldn't have been giving anyone advice; remember she's wounded. Have you been around negative people? That energy is bad. It will drain you.

Furthermore, Naomi confirms it wasn't about them; it was about her in (Ruth 1:13)

The latter part of Ruth 1:13 NIV

"No, my daughters. It is more bitter for me than for you, because the Lord's hand has turned against me!"

I'm going to say this once again. We can't allow anyone to talk us out of our blessings. You must discern the spirit behind the person. Several other characteristics can be a hindrance, for example, pride, jealousy, envy, strife those things that are fleshly. Throughout our lives, not everything will be peaches and cream. We must remain optimistic there will be both advantages and disadvantages. That doesn't mean we should give up and not press forward. Don't miss your opportunities, trying to avoid obstacles. We are going to face some challenges. We can't allow the fear of going through them to hinder our purpose. God's Word declares there will be *Trouble John 16:33, Persecution 2 Timothy 3:12* and *Affliction Psalms 34:19* His Word says He will deliver us from them all (Psalm 34:17.) Another example of someone persevering through trouble found in Acts 21, read on.

Acts 21:10-14 NIV

"After we had been there a number of days, a prophet named Agabus came down from Judea. Coming over to us, he took Paul's belt, tied his own hands and feet with it and said, The Holy Spirit

says, 'In this way the Jewish leaders in Jerusalem will bind the owner of this belt and will hand him over to the Gentiles.' When we heard this, we and the people there pleaded with Paul not to go up to Jerusalem. Then Paul answered, why are you weeping and breaking my heart? I am ready not only to be bound, but also to die in Jerusalem for the name of the Lord Jesus. When he would not be dissuaded, we gave up and said, The Lord's will be done."

"When you reach an obstruction, don't turn back, make another plan."

– Dr. Myles Munroe.

PRINCIPLE OF WAITING

Ruth 1:14 NIV

"At this they wept aloud again. Then Orpah kissed her mother-in-law goodbye, but Ruth clung to her."

I believe the key to Oprah's decision to turn back was contingent on the two questions Naomi asked. If she gave birth to sons, would you wait until they grew up? Would you remain unmarried for them? Unfortunately, the waiting process is one of the principles that lead us into making poor decisions. As a result, there is a high percentage of women in unsatisfactory marriages that are not God's will for their lives. This issue continues to contribute to a high divorce rate, unfortunately. This testimony I will never forget, and I will always make sure I tell it.

I took a class with a powerful Woman of God. When she spoke, you could feel God's presence. In this class was a group of ladies of varying ages. One day God inspired her to give her testimony about her marriage. She said God told her before she had gotten married to him, he was indeed her husband. God also told her not to marry him yet; wait because he is not ready. God still had to do some work in his character. Guess what she did? Disobeyed God and married him anyway. She had to suffer; he abused her and her children. He didn't have any respect for her or the call on her life. God gave her a church, and he took it from her. He would talk badly about her in public and on his live broadcast. He would degrade women in general, and he took that woman through Hell. She said to our class of women that she shared her testimony in hopes that we could avoid what she went through. She encouraged us to wait on God. By this time, I experience divorce twice.

What she said resonated within my spirit, and I've been trying to live by this principle ever since. The year 2020 makes 14 years of celibacy. Not in and of myself, but by the grace of God. Back in the day, one of the mothers at a church told me. He (God) will keep you if you desire to be maintained. God controls time! He has the power to slow it down, speed it up and cause it to come to a complete halt. Everything God desires for your life happens in His timing. We cannot manipulate God to do things sooner than His purpose. However, you have a choice as the lady did whether to wait on Him or not. I don't know if you've ever heard of the terms "Divine Will" or Permissive Will." God's Divine Will means of, from, or like God. God's Permissive Will is something He disapproves of or forbids but will allow if you persist. Even though He refuses, your eagerness overrides His will for you, He will grant it, and the consequences that come with it.

Proverbs 10:22 KJV

"The blessings of the Lord, it maketh rich, and he adds no sorrow."

Proverbs 10:22 NIV

"The blessing of the Lord brings wealth without painful toil.

He is not only speaking about monetarily; rich in health, family, relationships, marriage, peace, in all aspects of your life; with no sorrow. He wants us to experience His Divine Will as well as pursue it. For us to accomplish this, we must apply the principle of waiting. Not only are we to wait. It is equally important how we wait on God.

Psalms 27:14 NIV (David writes:)

"Wait for the Lord; be strong and take heart and wait for the Lord." Another translation KJV says, "wait on the Lord and be of good courage wait, I say on the Lord."

David expresses how we should wait by not murmuring and complaining, with good courage. Good courage comes by way of trusting God (See: Proverbs 3:5-6.) That reminds me of this song: "I Don't Mind Waiting On You Lord" Truth be told, most of us have a problem with waiting. When we don't wait on God, we forfeit our blessing. Like the lady, we spoke about earlier, me and maybe some of you had that thought in the back of your minds, especially when our way doesn't work. We were wondering what if? What if I had waited on God? What would have been my outcome? Subsequently, the principle of waiting is a learned behavior fortified through many prayers, Faith, Patience, and discipline.

Most importantly you must believe in the author: Jesus Christ (Hebrews 12:2) and the process. I want to encourage you to wait as someone helped me. (See James 1:4, 1 Corinthians 5:7, Galatians 5:22, Hebrews 11:1. James 2:20.)

Isaiah 40:28-31 KJV

"Hast thou not known? Hast thou not heard, that the everlasting God, the Lord, The Creator of the ends of the earth, fainteth not, neither is weary? there is no searching of His understanding. He giveth power to the faint; and to them that have no might He increases their strength; Even the youths shall faint and be weary, and the young men shall utterly fall: But they that wait on The Lord shall renew their strength; they shall mount up with wings as eagles; they shall run, and not be weary; and they shall walk, and not faint."

"DON'T FORFEIT YOUR BLESSING; wait on the Lord."

CHAPTER 3

PURPOSE DRIVEN: THE LORD'S WILL BE DONE

Understand that individuals with a purpose-driven life have unexplainable resilience and perseverance. It's bigger than your feelings, emotions, what's convenient, and what you can see with the natural eye. It's higher than your friends, your family, your foes, and even yourself. There is a yes in your spirit, but you don't know what you're saying yes too. You can't rationalize it. You just keep pushing towards it. Giving up is not within you because giving up is not an option. For example, in the past, my sister and I didn't have a relationship that was on excellent terms.

My mother had become extremely ill. She had been in poor health as long as I can remember. Subsequently, however, this was different; she had bone cancer. My sister was her caretaker. Her condition had miraculously gone into remission at this time. However, my sister spent the majority of her time at my mother's home. Also, God would put it on my heart quite frequently to visit my mother. It was a challenge, and I consequently wouldn't go. I wouldn't ignore Him, I would simply offer some excuse for why I couldn't go. I would only see her on my terms and at my own house. I was trying to avoid confrontation with my sister. I don't like conflict, and I was tired, as I was recently coming out of an abusive relationship. I was weary of fighting with people. I just wanted peace.

To worsen the matter, my mother would complain about my kids. I simply didn't want to deal with it. Problems escalated, I started having issues with paying my rent and lost my apartment. I was trying to do everything possible to prevent me from going to live with my mother. Reluctantly, I had to return home to live with her. My sister thought I had lost my mind. She said to me, "What is wrong with you? I've never seen you like this." She called me a slacker and some other names. Every time she would come over, she took the opportunity to offend me. I could have conjured up a few choice words, but God wouldn't allow me to say anything. I didn't have it in me anyway after what I had just gone through. As a result, she began to ease up a little bit.

Proverbs 16:7 (KJV)

"When a man's ways please the Lord, He maketh even his enemies to be at peace with him."

I didn't fully understand why I was there. Have you ever been to a place and asked yourself, "Why am I here?" At any rate, every morning, when I awakened, I would sit on my mother's sofa in her living room and read my Bible. As I prayed, God took me to this chapter in the Bible: Matthew 15.

Matthew 15:3-7 NIV

Jesus replied, "And why do you break the command of God for the sake of your tradition? For God said, 'Honor your father and mother and 'Anyone who curses his father or mother is be put to death.' But you say that if anyone declares that what might have been used to help their father or mother is 'devoted to God,' they are not to 'honor their father or mother' with it. Thus you nullify the word of God for the sake of your tradition. You hypocrites! Isaiah was right when he prophesied about you:"

He continued taking me there every morning when I woke up until I got it. I was the hypocrite; my mother's condition had her weak. Every morning she would get up, make herself a sausage, egg, and muffin with coffee, and read her Bible at the kitchen table. This one morning, after reading Matthew 15 for the 20th time, God had me look at her in that kitchen. She was weak, barely moving. My mother wasn't the same lady that would be fussing all the time. She didn't have the strength to fuss; I saw this once strong woman become so fragile. Resentment had me selfish and blind to the needs of my mother. I wouldn't have seen this if I wasn't living with her. The next morning, I made my mother's breakfast. I continued to make her breakfast, serving her became an honor, as *Matthew 15:3 states*.

Much had transpired in that year; I lived with her. God came to me in a dream and told me that my mother wasn't going to be here much longer. He also told me there were going to be a lot of deaths that year, and in 2009 it was. However, when I woke up, I immediately called my sisters and told them what God had said. "Momma is not going to be here much longer, spend as much time as you can with her." God began to deal with me even more regarding my mother. He told me that she had unforgiveness in her heart. One morning, she got up as usual with her daily routine. I asked her, no first I told her what God said and then I asked her who it was that she hadn't forgiven. She told me it was my Father! That blew my mind! She had been holding that unforgiveness in her heart towards my Father for over 40 years. She had unforgiveness for others, but he was the root of her unforgiveness. I told her, "Mama, you have got to let him go for you to be free. More importantly, for you to go to heaven." We discussed her reasons for holding that resentment in her heart for so long. Then we begin to pray, she struggled for a while, and we start to press in more intently. The Holy Spirit filled the room. My mother started to speak in tongues and crying out to God. At that point, it was Him and her I got out of it. She and God went on for a while. A peace came over her as she released it. That's when I realized that was my sole purpose for being there. God is so awesome; He orchestrated the whole thing. He wouldn't allow my sister's resentment toward me and my reluctance to return to my mother's house, to prevent me from filling my purpose. God didn't even allow my mother's resentment to prevent her from going to heaven. It was 6-months after He told me she wasn't going to be here long, cancer returned, and she passed away. This day was the saddest day of my life because I loved my mother dearly. God told me, however, "not more than I love her." I couldn't argue with that. I told Him I'm going to miss her. I thank God He didn't allow me to miss the opportunity to spend that crucial time with my mother. Purpose disrupts your plans, impacts, controls, and rearranges your entire life. When you're purpose-driven, it is not about you; it's about your purpose. *Some opportunities only come once.*

Ruth

Ruth's journey was extraordinary. Ruth's yes to the waiting process changed the course of her life (*Ruth 1:16*.) The principle of waiting enabled her to experience the life that most women dreams. She married Boaz, the most sought out, eligible bachelor and one of the richest men in Bethlehem Judah. She became famous; her fame went throughout Bethlehem; through marriage and the birth of her son Obed, who is in the lineage of Jesus Christ (*Matthew 1:5*.) Obed is Jesse's Father, who is King David's Father. This marriage places her in the royal family as one of the great grandmothers of our Lord and Savior Jesus Christ.

Romans 15:12 (NIV)

And again, Isaiah says, "The Root of Jesse will spring up, one who will arise to rule over the nations; in Him, the Gentiles will hope."

Our children's, children's, children, and so on will hear about Ruth. You think that's awesome, but the most profound thing to me in her experience, she didn't ask for it or pray for it. This life was the life God planned for her (*Jeremiah 29:11*.) Those of us that are in the waiting process ought to be getting excited right about here. Someone once quoted:

"If we follow in the direction of the Creator, our lives will have meaning and purpose. When we follow in the opposite direction of the Creator, it will be empty of meaning and purpose."

These are the famous words that catapulted Ruth to her destiny, motivated by her purpose:

Ruth 1:16-17 (NIV)

But Ruth replied, "Don't urge me to leave you or to turn back from you. Where you go, I will go, and where you stay, I will stay. Your people will be my people and your God my God." Where you die, I will die, and there I will be buried. May the Lord deal with me, be it ever so severely, if even but death separates you and me."

What was Ruth's motivation?

It should be evident by now that Ruth's inspiration and motivation came directly from God's purpose for her. However, we also have a part of fulfilling. That part is our motivation. Everyone's motivation is not coming from a holy place. People are motivated by a plethora of things. Money, fame, finances, notoriety, and selfish ambition, etc., In fact, I can safely say this is with the majority of individuals considering we are in the last days.

2 Timothy 3:1-4 (NIV)

"But mark this: There will be terrible times in the last days. People will be lovers of themselves, lovers of money, boastful, proud, abusive, disobedient to their parents, ungrateful, unholy, without love, unforgiving, slanderous, without self-control, brutal, not lovers of the good, treacherous, rash, conceited, lovers of pleasure rather than lovers of God."

Our intentions derive from a place in our hearts either from a Godly or ungodly. From a place of love or void of love, selfish or unselfish, good or evil as we discussed earlier flesh and spirit. The intent of our hearts judges us.

1 Samuel 16:7 (NIV)

"But the Lord said to Samuel, do not consider his appearance or his height, for I have rejected him. The Lord does not look at the things man looks at. Man looks at the outward appearance, but The Lord looks at the heart."

People can say and do things that seem right, however, with the wrong intention. God is not concerned with the things we do more so than why and how we do them. As an example, God can make good things come out of a bad situation. As a result of being homeless, I became more passionate about others that are in unfortunate and similar circumstances. I was homeless for about three years but didn't realize it because I had food to eat and a roof over my head. I was living in an extended-stay hotel, which qualified my family and me as being homeless. I found that out when I went to register my children for school. However, homelessness was right for me. It put gratefulness and compassion in my heart that I probably wouldn't have had if I hadn't experienced it. As a result, I wrote my first book when I was homeless. It also took me to another level of faith in God. Sometimes it got a little rough paying the hotel bill every week. Not to mention that one time I didn't have the money. I exhausted all my resources; it was indeed a trying of my faith. My struggle was leaning to my understanding. Trying to figure out how I was, or God was going to do it. I indeed battled with that! I knew that was one of the reasons I kept going through because I didn't pass that test. I had made up in my mind, not this time. I was going to get through this test. I went into the bathroom, which was my prayer closet and cried out to the Lord. I asked the Lord to help me not get in my way. I said, "Lord, I'm just going to trust you. If I have to get out, I'll just get put out; I'm leaving it up to you." I was mentally exhausted about this time. I didn't ask anybody; I didn't put my hands in it as I would typically do. I came out of the bathroom, sat on the bed, and began to watch television. It had gotten late, I was expecting the office to call and ask for a payment. I didn't hear from the office. I went to bed woke up the next morning, got my children on the bus for school. I started my day on the prayer line; the day went by, my children had returned from school, I still didn't hear from the office. It had gotten late we went to sleep this was the second day. This happened consistently for 5 days, 5 signifies grace. However, on that sixth day I received a phone call from the office. The lady said, "Miss Taylor your room is due." Mind you I still didn't have the money, she wasn't mean, she just told me it was due and hung up. No one came to put me out, I just began packing my stuff I knew it was time to go. I simply didn't know where we were going. God always has a ram in the bush. I called Miss Janice, who was a Godsend. I met her while I was staying in the first hotel we stayed in when we first came to Norcross Georgia. God rest her soul. She came and picked us up. Miss Janet knew my situations Miss Janet would call daily and check on us. "You alright," she would say. I would answer "Yes Miss Janice, we are alright, we're still here". I believe she was anticipating my call. However, when she picked us up, she offered us to stay with her. She only had a room with one king-size bed in It, my daughter and I made a pallet on the floor, and my son slept in the bed with Miss Janice. God had allowed me and my children to stay in that room for five days without paying, and then He put it on Miss Janice's heart to enable us to stay with her. God will make a way; it may not be conventional. I'm not going to lie. It was a painful and humbling experience, but it was for my good. In the process of my homelessness, it gave me awareness. God allowed me to see some things, a corrupt system, and dishonest people. An organization that takes advantage and exploits those with disadvantages for their selfish gain. A vast amount of these organizations that are government-funded and nonprofit. And even some of the churches are not providing the services that they are getting funded. I experienced the magnitude of this firsthand. I know how it feels; taken advantage of when you're in a crisis. To sign your name on the sign-in sheet, fill out the paperwork, even go as far as taking my picture, and still not receive any help. It felt molested because I knew they were going to get credit for something they didn't do. I know how it feels to be rejected by people that have the means to help you. God had me go through that for a reason, to expose the system, people, and myself. In a time of crisis, you will see who's there for you. Where were the love and the compassion of God? God showed me where He was, in that little old feisty lady, Miss Janice. She went above and beyond to extend herself, sacrificing her comfort, to share a room she purchased with just herself in mind, with myself and my children.

Matthew 6:1 (NIV)

"Be careful not to do your' acts of righteousness' before men, to be seen by them. If you do, you will have no reward from your Father in heaven."

Paul tells the Church of Philippi in **Philippians 2:1-5** to be like-minded as Christ:

• Same in Love

• Being of one Spirit

• Purpose

• Humility

He admonishes them to do nothing out of:

• Selfish ambition

• Vain conceit

Do these things out of humility, considering others better than yourselves. He goes on to tell them each of you should not be concerned with your interests, but also your concern should be for the benefit of others. Our attitude should be the same as Christ Jesus, who humbled Himself even unto death on the cross. Furthermore, Ruth's motivation wasn't self-centered neither was Miss Janice's. Ruth's reason for going with Naomi was likeminded, as was Christ's, unselfish love.

Ruth 4:15 NIV (latter clause)

"... For your daughter-in-law who loves you and who is better to you than seven sons, has given him birth."

. . .

"Good deeds with the wrong motives are not good deeds. If you're not doing it in love and obedience, you're doing it in vain."

PRINCIPLE OF LOVE

Love is God

1 John 4:7-8 (NIV)

"Dear friends, let us love one another, for love comes from God. Everyone who loves has been born of God. Whoever does not love does not know God, because God is love."

The principle of love is to love God and love one another. Which is the most excellent command given to the believers (See: Mark 12:29-31.) Jesus says there is no commandment greater than these. Love is why we have the opportunity of eternal life *(See: John 3:16.)* God's intention was obvious. He so loved the world that He gave His only begotten Son. His motivation wasn't driven or subjected to any conditions; in fact, His reasons are unconditional. What determines unconditional love, action (works), time, and change. By action, because love is an action word. Love gives, sacrifices is patient, kind, and serves, among other things. (See: 1 Corinthians 13:4-8) Our primary example is Jesus. Time brings about a change; change is inevitable; the only one who doesn't change is God. Some change is for the better, some for the worse; in health, finances, looks, etc.

Consequently, love will be put to the test through trials and tribulations. This will be the deciding factor whether it's conditional or unconditional. If the conditions change, will love remain? All the more reason you should take your time to learn people. What people do consistently that's who they are. When someone shows you who they are believe them. I made this mistake in the past, and I ignored some apparent and consistent behavior in my past relationships. As a result, it caused me pain and grief that could have been avoided. Understand, I take full responsibility for my part, because the signs were there. They didn't force me to choose them. I'm not making any excuses for myself, but I didn't understand it at the time; I was grieving the absence of my Father. However, being void of a relationship with him caused me to be angry, rebellious, and unfamiliar with what love looked like from a man. Rebellion and anger will affect your decision-making ability; consequently, affecting a positive outcome. Now I know what a man should look like: God. I was associating love with a feeling. We don't feel God's love; we see the results of God's love. If we went solely by emotions, we would be confused, to be honest. Sometimes in this walk as a believer, it doesn't always feel good. However, we know it's working for our good.

Moreover, a man can make you feel good and not love you. It goes back to the intentions of what his motives are? Why is he with you in the first place? Or why are you with him? Again, for myself it goes back to me grieving my Father. Were my intentions for being with them because I loved them? No, or was I looking for a father? Yes, I can honestly say I didn't. Love begins with God and then yourself. I couldn't love them because I didn't love myself. I had a love/hate relationship with them. As I said previously, they were three depictions of my Father: an alcoholic, a cheater, and one who perpetrated both mental and physical abuse, this is who my Father was to my mother. My only point of reference. People often use the term LOVE so loosely. It's a thin line between love and lust. Being in-love is often associated with passion, infatuation, instability, and conditions.

Conditions are meeting requirements and terms. As soon as the condition change, they have fallen out of love. What has taken place is, the thing (condition) that they fell in love with has changed. When that happens, you're useless to them. Some examples of terms people are attracted to physical appearance, figure, cooking abilities, material things, financial status, social status, etc., and those relationships are short-lived, stop cooking, lose that shape and see what happens? They are on to the next victim. As for me, I found true love in God, and I will not compromise myself with any relationship, be it with friends, relatives, or marriage. I advise you to allow God to show you what love is, and then you won't have a distorted view. As a result, you will be able to navigate your relationships from His example. Just as important, the next time someone says they love you, let it be proven by their actions (works), not a feeling, for example like Boaz.

Love is unfailing. And it is proven by the test of time.

1 Corinthians 13:13 (NIV)

"And now these three remain faith, hope, and love. But the greatest of these is love."

"Principles guarantee success. *A principle is a law which works everywhere, it works for anyone, and it works anytime, in every situation*" – Dr. Myles Monroe

BOAZ'S ATTRACTION TO RUTH

As we discussed in earlier chapters, God responds to His principles. Ruth was from a foreign place, but she lived by principles, which also gave her access to God's blessings. The tenets of servitude, humility, faith, obedience, patience, just to name a few. Boaz recognized these qualities in Ruth, and God responded to them. As Dr. Miles Munroe stated, principles guarantee success. If we want to have abundant success in health, relationships, and finances, we must learn these principles and apply them. Her principles set her apart from other female servants who became an attraction to all the people, but more importantly, to Boaz.

Ruth 2:10-12 (NIV)

"At this, she bowed down her face to the ground. She exclaimed, why have I found such favor in your eyes that you notice me a foreigner? Boaz replied I've been told all about what you have done for your mother-in-law since the death of your husband how you left your father and mother and your homeland and came to live with a people you did not know before."

Consequently, also, Ruth's yes cost her something as Boaz acknowledges her heritage, her relatives, her culture, and her God. She left everything in her past to step into the unknown. Her past set the stage for her future. To take possession of new territory, we can't be afraid to take risks.

Two of the Principle Rules for Success God gave to Joshua was to be strong and courageous. (*See: Joshua 1.*) To get something different, we must be willing to do something different. Your future awaits on the other side of unconventional. Statistics say women outnumber men in the world. That means men have more options to choose from than women. What is it that makes you different from other women? It's not your body parts because we all have the same thing. It is what made Ruth different, and Boaz takes notice.

Ruth 3:10-11 (KJV)

"And he said, Blessed be thou of the Lord, my daughter: for thou hast shewed more kindness in the latter end than at the beginning, inasmuch as thou followedst not young men, whether poor or rich. And now, my daughter, fear not; I will do to thee all that thou requirest: for all the city of my people doth know that thou art a virtuous woman."

Ruth's standards made her stand out; she was a virtuous woman. There are two types of women noble and wayward, and a virtuous woman is elusive; she is rare. In Proverbs 31, it says she is hard to find. Her worth is far more than rubies, meaning she is valuable (*See: Chapter 6.*) Being a woman of virtue adds value to your life. Any woman can be a wife because she holds the title of a woman.

However, every woman doesn't possess the qualities to be a wife. Quality is what adds value to a woman. It's the difference between the finest champagne and beer. Men will treat you based on what you believe your worth is. You must know your value. Boaz wasn't evasive, he saw the quality of woman Ruth was, and his intentions toward her were honorable. May I point out, it didn't have anything to do with her finances or material accomplishments because she didn't have any. He had the opportunity to defile her body and character, and she was alone with him all night. However, he didn't, he covered her. He protected her name and reputation; it was a demonstration of his character and his respect for her. His attitude came from her having respect for herself. As a result, he told her to lay at his feet until morning, then leave early so no one will see her. Just as important, he didn't allow her to go empty-handed. He gave her food to take back for her and Naomi while she WAITED. Take this into consideration. A man can only do what we as women allow him to do.

We must know who we are and who's we are. Being a child of God is your greatest asset (value). Again, as I said earlier, know your worth. Love and respect begin with us loving and respecting ourselves first. When a man sees that you have uncompromising standards, either he will abide by them or leave. Boaz did the honorable thing, even if it meant he had to deny his flesh and honor her. If he is a man from God, also though they have desires, he will do the right thing and wait until marriage. More importantly, you must believe that you are worth waiting for and not give up on your standards. I wish I knew then what I know now, fleshly-driven relationships can get us in a lot of trouble. Trouble is easy to get in and not so easy to get out. In this flesh dwells no good thing. The flesh doesn't want to do right; it is an enemy of God and His principles. It produces death; it will lead one to a dead end. Anyhow, to sum it all up, Boaz did everything decent to redeem Ruth legally. He married her, and there you have it; Ruth and Boaz's happily ever after. However, she didn't accomplish it by herself without the help and wisdom of her mother-in-law Naomi.

Proverbs 15:22 KJV

"Without counsel, purposes are disappointed: but in the multitude of counselors they are established."

Naomi's Purpose

Briefly, but importantly Naomi was a wise woman in her own right which added value to her. Ruth didn't have the wisdom that Naomi had, but she was willing and obedient to follow her instructions. That is the number one sign of a great leader: a follower. Not saying you should follow everything and everybody. Like we discussed previously, God will put some influential people in our lives to guide us to our purpose. As a result, she had trust and respect for Naomi. This is another key to the principle Rules of Success. God gave Joshua; to obey His (law) which means instructions in Hebrew translation. God uses the word then, which is a conditional word. Then when you follow His direction, you will be prosperous and successful wherever you go. (*See: Joshua Chapter 1.*) This is the problem we have with the younger generation they don't want to listen to wise instruction. A significant reason for this is many older women are out of place. The former is supposed to teach the young. This was Paul's instruction to Titus in the Book of Titus 2. In order to teach younger people, the elder must live by example. It's hard to get someone to believe in something that's not working for you. People want to see results.

Moreover, we were discussing adding value to your life; wisdom also adds value to a person's life. Good judgment comes by experience, and experience is an excellent teacher. Experience is what qualified me, not because I had a great success; it's because I survived. When I was going through my divorce from my second husband, it was a painful, tormenting experience. I was in constant mental distress. I thought I was going to lose my mind. One day it had gotten so bad I went into the bathroom in my apartment; my prayer closet was always my bathroom. Anyway, I went in there, and I asked God why I was going through this? He said to me, tenderly, I will never forget it; "It's not for you, it's for somebody else." I immediately got quiet, and a peace came over me as God comforted me to go on through. Rest assured, if God doesn't send a tangible person to help you, God's Holy Spirit is always there to guide you through. I don't know where I would be without Him, our precious Holy Spirit! Everything we go through has a purpose, good or bad.

You can stay bitter and allow it to continue to have power over you.

Or you can take your control back, learn from it, and use it as an opportunity to help someone else. Your testimony has an audience. Naomi received her power back. She was purposed to be a valuable asset to the progression of Ruth's success because of her wisdom. If she had of remained bitter and disobedient, not only would she had of blocked Ruth's blessings, she would have prevented her own. Furthermore, if you want to be successful, you must humble yourself and learn how to follow wise counsel. God has given us the keys to unlock heaven's vault to our blessings, and one of those keys is being obedient to the process. And you to can have your Ruth and Boaz experience it's worth waiting for.

Ruth 4:14-15 (KJV)

"And the women said to Naomi, Blessed be the Lord, which hath not left thee this day without a kinsman, that his name may be famous in Israel. And he shall be unto thee a restorer of thy life, and a nourisher of thy old age: for thy daughter in law, which loveth thee, which is better to thee than seven sons, hath born him."

DO YOU KNOW WHO YOU'RE CARRYING?

In summation, how does purpose manifest in the earth? From the mother's womb. The purpose is birthed out of the womb naturally then spiritually. The Bible says the natural came before the spiritual (1 Corinthians 15:46.) The spirit needs a body to accomplish its purpose in the earth (Spirit of God or the spirit of Satan). All humanity came from a woman. God told Sarah that Kings of people would come from her womb (*See: Genesis 17:15.*) Purpose means a reason for which something is done or created or for which something exists. This two-fold definition applies to us as a people and everything God created. He created all things for a purpose; no one is here by mistake. We are a purpose with a purpose. The first purpose you must find is yourself and know that you are significant. Get to know and love yourself, likes, and dislikes.

Additionally, find out why God purposed you here; it may be what your passion. Ruth's purpose for existence did not center on a vocation or a career. It didn't have anything to do with her education, social status, or financial status. These are things people and society believe make them essential. These are things you acquire, they don't define who you are. Unbeknownst to her, Ruth's purpose was in her womb another example, Mary the mother of Jesus. Not every woman will experience natural childbirth some women will be a midwife. Like Naomi, her wisdom equipped her to assist in developing Ruth's purpose. As for Ruth, as well as the rest of us, our objective God established before we were in our mother's womb (*Jeremiah 1:4-5.*) Concerning Jeremiah's encounter, some of us will not have the same privilege as Jeremiah, where God comes to you in an audible voice and tells you your purpose. Some of us like Ruth, will find it out by being led by His Spirit. That's why we must be very cautious with putting God in a box. Saying He's going to do it this way or that way. He's going to do His way, period! He is past finding out (*Isaiah 55:8-9.*)

"The Lord's Will be done."

CHAPTER 4

WHAT SUCCESSFUL PEOPLE HAVE IN COMMON

I have done extensive research on successful people, someone told me if you want to be successful, get in the minds of successful people.

If you want to be successful, don't seek success. Make yourself valuable -Dr. Myles Munroe

Dr. Myles Munroe:

1. Success is not a pursuit

2. Success is discovering what you were born to do

3. Success is dying empty

4. Success is a result of obedience to the law

I'm certainly not holding a man at a higher esteem than God. My purpose was to display the results through man from those that have applied godly principles. Hands down, the most exceptional leader and the most successful person ever to walk this earth, in all categories, is Jesus Christ. He has the most significant influence, and He made the greatest sacrifice, Jesus has the highest purpose, He is the greatest giver and the most excellent servant, etc. He's the most famous person in the world. In my eyes, Jesus Christ is the only star. I'm not pursuing stardom; I just want to be impactful. Despite all the adverse things He endured, He didn't give up! Most importantly, success has different levels He (Jesus) reached the highest level of success because He finished the work. He left here empty. For example, a successful marriage is a marriage that fulfills its commitment to death do us part. Our unions, our purpose, or anything we set out to do for that matter, must be worth taking your last breath. Even though we were not worthy of dying for, Jesus took His last breath for us. Furthermore, since this story centers on Ruth, she told Naomi where you die, I will die; there I will be buried. She was determined to take her last breath to follow Naomi. Take a minute and think about it, is what you're doing and who you're with worth taking your last breath? If you have any reluctance, you may not be in or executing your purpose. You need to reevaluate and do an assessment of your life. Dr. Myles Munroe, in his teaching, he says, these five questions control the human race. If you are going to be successful, you must know them. These five questions also can frustrate the human race if you don't know them:

1. Who am I?

2. Where am I from?

3. Why am I here?

4. What can I do?

5. Where am I going, my destination?

If you know them, you are on the right road. If you don't, it will be tragic because, without purpose, our lives have no meaning. That's one of the reasons why the suicide rate is so high, especially in the younger generation. We are taught many subjects in school, but not about purpose, it was non-disclosed information. We will have more discussion on this later (See: *Chapter 5*.) However, as a result, I discovered in those that have reached a level of success, they have several commonalities. They have found the thing worth taking their last breath for; their purpose, some call it niche. The late, great Dr. Martin Luther King, Jr., quoted: "No one knows why they are alive until they know what they'd die for."

From Multi-Millionaires to Billionaires, Biblical and Practical, they have unlocked the doors to success. All by using the proper keys. Some of them we have already discussed in the previous chapters. I want to share a few more key principles and their benefits with you. Subsequently, that will help you live a successful life in your relationships, health, and finances. Not to say that we will not face challenges, that's part of life. As a result of the life of Jesus, we can live in this life and live in it more abundantly, all because Jesus finished His assignment (See: John 10:10.)

"If you want what I have, you have to do what I did. Put God first!" – Denzel Washington

THE NUMBER ONE *Key to Success: Putting God First!* Jesus said if we seek the Kingdom first and His righteousness, all these things will be added unto us. We must put things in their right perspective, as Denzel Washington says, put God first! Also, change our pursuit instead of pursuing success, stuff, and ideas, seek the Kingdom and His righteousness. Dr. Myles Munroe said if you're obedient to the law of success, you won't have to chase success. Success will be chasing you. The first and the most critical principle, alongside believing in Him, is God having preeminence in our lives. Putting Him first guarantees access to all His benefits.

Matthew 6:33 (KJV)

"But seek ye first the kingdom of God and His righteousness, and all these things shall be added unto you."

Psalm 103: 1-5 NIV

"Praise the Lord, O my soul; all my inmost being, praise His holy

name. Praise the Lord, O my soul, and forget not all His benefits who forgives all your sins and HEALS all your diseases, who redeems your life from the pit and crowns you with love and compassion, who satisfies your desires with good things so that your youth is renewed like the eagle's."

"Live to service" – Will Smith

Number Two: Serving. We should seek to do things that God values, and one of them is serving. Jesus said I didn't come to be served; I came to be a servant and give my life ransom for many. Doing things for others adds value to you as well as to someone else. A servant is the highest calling one can attain, with the most significant rewards. The Bible declares in Mark 10:44, "… the Chiefest shall be a servant of all." Martin Luther King, Jr., quoted: "Everybody can be great because anybody can serve. You don't have to make your subject and verb agree to serve. You only need a heart full of grace. A soul generated by love." Servitude is also produced from the principle law of giving, giving of yourself. Giving is not a one-track thing; most people associate giving with money only. Giving has many categories, for example, the Bible says when we give it will be given unto us in full measure, pressed down, shaken together, and running over will men give unto your bosoms. Most people use this scripture out of context and with the wrong intention to persuade people out of their money. However, Jesus was speaking about other categories as well, loving your enemies, being merciful, non-judgmental, not condemning others, forgiving, and lending to others. However, when you give, it will be given back to you. That's the universal system God has created in the earth. God calls it seedtime and harvest (see the scripture below.) What a man sows, (the seeds he plants) he will also reap. What you put in the universe good, bad, or indifferent; will come back to you. As you see, we can be our own worst enemy or our greatest success. God has left it up to us to determine our outcome by the choices we make.

Genesis 8:22 (KJV)

"While the earth remaineth, seedtime and harvest, and cold and heat, and summer and winter, and day and night shall not cease."

Galatians 6:7-8 (KJV)

"Be not deceived: God is not mocked: for whatsoever a man soweth, that shall he also reap. For he that soweth to his flesh shall of the flesh reap corruption, but he that soweth to the Spirit shall of the Spirit reap life everlasting."

Luke 6:38 (NIV)

"Give, and it will be given to you. A good measure, pressed down, shaken together and running over, will be poured into your lap. For with the measure you use, it will be measured to you."

"Life's most persistent question is, what are you doing for others?" – Dr. Martin Luther King, Jr.,

Meditate – Sean Combs

Number Three Meditation. The final Principle Rule of Success God gave Joshua in the Book Joshua Chapter 1 was meditation. To meditate on His laws, as we discussed earlier, means His instructions. The one I struggled with, setting aside time for reflection. Jesus, when He went to the Father and prayed, He prayed in this order. He prayed for Himself, His disciples and then He prayed for the other believers (*See: John 17.*) The majority of women tend to neglect themselves. We put everything and everybody before ourselves. Reality is, we can't be any good to anyone if we do not take care of ourselves first! We must commit to ourselves before we can commit to anyone else. Meditation is personal. It will build up our inner strength, mind, body, and soul and set the course of our day. Then we will be able to perform well, be useful, and successful in everything we put our hands to do. Program yourself to be successful by the Word of God, and in the areas, you would like to become successful. For example, meditate and see yourself as a good mother and wife, healed, wealthy, in your purpose, walking through every door of opportunity, in Jesus' Name. Meditation can also mean to declare. If you declare a thing, it will be established. Declare God's Word:

"I can do all things through Christ that strengthens me; I am more than a conquer in Christ Jesus, By His stripes, I am healed, I shall live and not die and declare the works of the Lord."

Psalm 37:4 (KJV)

"Delight thyself also in the Lord, and He shall give you thee the desires of thine heart."

I just want to reiterate this. We must make sure that even our meditation is done with the right motive; to see the best possible results! What is the right motivation? Merely the same thing He told Joshua: obedience motivated by love. However, I wish everything was as simple as just writing down something on a piece of paper, or me just telling you, and voila, done. For some people like myself, it wasn't that simple because I was a hardheaded, disobedient child, which carried over into my adulthood. It takes hard work, a made-up mind, and some spankings (rebukes,) to bring our lives under subjection to the authority of God.

Moreover, Jesus told the disciples: "If you love me, keep (obey) my commands. (See: John 14:15.) Additionally, obedience is better than sacrifice. (*1 Samuel 15:22-24*) When you build a relationship with God, His desires will become your desires, and your meditation will be in alignment with the Holy Spirit, and you won't be thinking amiss. More importantly, having the right motive will help our meditation become acceptable in His sight.

James 4:3 (NIV)

"When you ask, you do not receive, because you ask with wrong motives, that you may spend what you get on your pleasures."

Psalm 19:14 (KJV)

"Let the words of my mouth, and the meditation of my heart, be acceptable in thy sight, O Lord, my strength, and my redeemer."

Also, meditation will keep us focused, in alignment, and give us peace and clarity of God's Word. Meditation will change the negative battles and distractions that come and bring them into captivity. Meditation will transform our lives and bring us under subjection. It will train your mind to think on those things that are lovely, pure and of good report (*See: Philippians 4:8.*) I found the best time for me to meditate is in the morning before I get busy. When we seek Him early, the Bible says we will find Him. Dr. Myles Munroe said it like this; there are 24 hours in a day. God requires only 10%, which is 2 hours and 45 minutes. After all that God does for us surely, we can, at the very least, give Him 2 hours and 45 minutes of our time. I believe He is worthy of it, don't you? We must do it as if our lives depended on it because it does. The Bible says, man shall not live by bread alone, but by every word that proceeds out of the mouth of God (*See: Matthew 4:4.*) Faith comes by hearing the Word (*Romans 10:17.*) Meditation is a key to success and manifestation, see a couple of benefits in Joshua 1:8 as well as Psalm 1. (See also Isaiah 26:3, Matthew 6:6, and Psalm 119:15-16.)

Joshua 1:8 (NIV)

"Do not let this Book of Law (instructions) depart from your mouth: meditate on it day and night, so that you may be careful to do everything written in it. Then you will be prosperous and successful."

Psalms 1:3 (NIV)

"Blessed is the man who does not walk in the counsel of the wicked or stand in the way of sinners or sit in the seat of mockers. But his delight is in the law of the Lord, and on His law, he meditates day and night. He is like a tree planted by streams of water, which

yields its fruit in season and whose leaf does not wither. Whatever he does prospers."

"Everything I have is by the Grace of God" – Denzel Washington

Number Four: Humility. There are two types of humility true and false. Only God can measure the modesty of a man because He's the only one that knows our hearts. What the world calls humble is not humility to God. Subsequently, the world has its principles; such regulations have an appearance of wisdom, self-imposed worship, and a false humility (S*ee: Colossians 2:20.*) True humility is from God and begins within our minds. In Greek, the word is "**tapeinophorsune**" which means lowliness of human pride. Lowliness of mind. The mindset is having a low opinion of one's self, a deep sense of one's littleness. We are not to think of ourselves more highly than we ought, because it is by God's grace and mercy we are not consumed with the antics of this world. Humility is not something we are born with; it's a learned behavior and a choice. Honestly, all principles are learned behaviors. That's why the Bible tells us to humble ourselves. In other words, practice humility. Also, this lets us know we have the power to do so if we choose. We have the most exceptional example, Jesus! He is the epitome of humility. He humbled Himself and became obedient to death. As a result, God exalted Him to the highest place and gave Him the name above all names (See: Philippians 2:11.) As was discussed earlier, Apostle Paul says in that same chapter, our attitude should be the same as Jesus. Denzel Washington says if we want the same results, we must do what He did! For example, when we were in school, the teacher presented the lesson, but it was up to us to learn it and apply it. God takes us through the same process. He gives us the manual for life; the Bible, which is, by the way, the most excellent motivational, transformational, inspirational, and informative book in the world. And God gave us many teachers; however, God's not forcing us to read it or receive it. He made the Bible and the teachers available; it is up to us to learn, get the tools we need, and apply them accordingly. Also, it all depends on how you see life, life is full of learning opportunities, and some people just keep "skipping school" as my son says. We must know we are always in school. The school of life is still in session! Furthermore, humility adds value and recognition to our lives. It produces grace, honor, character, and elevation.

James 4:10 (NIV)

"Humble yourselves before the Lord, and He will lift you up."

James 4:6 (NIV)

"God opposes the proud but gives grace to the humble."

Proverbs 18:12 (NIV)

"Before a downfall the heart is haughty, but humility comes before honor."

1 Peter 5:6 (NIV)

"Humble yourselves, therefore under God's mighty hand, that He may lift you up in due time."

"PEOPLE FAIL TO ACHIEVE MASTERY, **not because they are not talented, but because they aren't disciplined"**

– Daniel Pink

There are a lot of talented and gifted people in the world that are nonproductive. Talents and gifts are not enough in and of themselves to achieve success. We see gifted people on the streets and in the subway, begging for money. We recognize talented people that are alcoholics, addicted to drugs, prostitutes, etc., talented people are working in dead-end jobs that they despise, showing up every day. Some will never discover because they haven't mastered these attributes. Mastering these attributes help take us to the next level.

• Master Discipline

- Master Consistency
- Master Prioritizing
- Master your Faith walk
- Master your prayer life

Things to Eliminate:

- Complaining
- Procrastination
- Unbelief
- Fear
- Self-doubt

"It's the quality, not the longevity of one's life that's important." – Dr. Martin Luther King, Jr.,

CHAPTER 5

WHY GOD CREATED WOMAN: FROM THE BEGINNING

ho am I?

"I am a child of God" – Oprah Winfrey

As a result of my relationship with God, prayer, His Word, and the guidance of the Holy Spirit, I know who I am. I am a child of God! Many have suffered from identity. Oprah Winfrey was interviewing Maya Angelou, who was such a profound and influential woman of God. When she spoke, people listened. Oprah looked at Maya Angelou as one of her mentors for wisdom and life lessons. In one of her conversations with Oprah, I can't remember exactly the words that lead up to this. However, she said to Oprah; you are a child of God. As a result, Oprah gave a commencement speech at Spelman College in 2012. The lady who introduced Oprah at this event shares the reason behind Oprah's success. Her success accredited wasn't to her career as a broadcaster, her television talk show, the Movie: "The Color Purple," the credit went to who she is, Oprah said success was her birthright as a child of God. Moreover, she began to speak on the three things she felt mattered, she quotes Maya Angelou: "Your crown is paid for, put it on your head and wear it." She goes on to say these three things will carry you if you let them:

- Knowing who you are:

And I quote, "I am God's child, I am that which is born of all that is. I am a spiritual being having a human experience. Because I am connected to the source of all that is, all that is possible is possible for me. That's who I am." – Oprah Winfrey

- WHAT DO I WANT?

And I quote, "I don't want to be just successful in the world. I don't want just to make a mark or have a legacy. The answer to that question for me is that I want to fulfill the highest, truest expression of myself as a human being. I want to fulfill the promise that the Creator dreamed when He dreamed the cells that made up me." – Oprah Winfrey

- YOU MUST FIND a way to serve:

And I quote, "Service and significance are that which you bring to your service, that's what's lasting. Whatever your talent, job, or occupation in service to the world. All the successful people in the world, whether they know it or not, they have that paradigm of service." – Oprah Winfrey

I'VE POSED this question to a group of people who are you? I asked them to go and look in the mirror and tell me who they see. Some said to me, myself, and some gave their name. Those answers are common, but it's not who you are. Do you realize there are an enormous amount of people that know their name but don't know who they are? I was one of them. Who are you? Your name is your identification, not who you are. Adam called Eve a woman before she received her name; a woman is not her identity. A woman is used to distinguish the difference between gender, whether male or female. We all are women; Adam says that's what we are called, I will call her woman. However, we are known by our unique name. For example, if you hear a child say "Momma" in a room full of mothers, all the mothers will answer or turn to look to see if that's their child. However, if someone calls you your name, you will answer because it identifies who you are as an individual. Not knowing who we are can also be confused with titles and the roles we play because we as women are a lot of things to a lot of people. To walk in our identity, we must understand why God created us.

"Become your best self; that's what makes you unique; it's what makes you special." – Tyler Perry

My beginning was traumatic due to the absence of my father. As a result, as I said in an earlier chapter, I was rebellious, disobedient, and hostile. My mother's disciplinary tactic was what most black parents used to correct bad behavior: whippings. Our ancestors inherited this tactic by way of slavery. Its usage was to provoke fear, control, and oppression in the black race. Consequently, all she accomplished in doing so was to create more hostility in me, which had a reflection on how I viewed her and the world. Subsequently, I came up at a time when we couldn't talk. We couldn't express ourselves, even if we were innocent, we had to shut up and take the punishment. My mother would say: "Are you calling me a liar?" In my mind, I would say the curse word and yes, because I was telling the truth. However, I knew the consequences that would follow if I said it out loud. She was going to knock me down on the floor. As a result, it forced me to suppress my feeling. Consequently, that angry child became an angry, confused adult. Fortunately, my mother knew God, and I finally realized she was doing what she knew to do. It was the same thing that was done to her. However, she made sure that we established a relationship with God. That's why it's essential to introduce our children to Jesus, just like The Word says:

Proverbs 22:6 (KJV)

"Train up a child in the way they should go: and when he is old, he will not depart from it."

My saving grace, back then, I couldn't even look in the mirror at myself, let alone declare who I was. I now realize if I would've looked in the mirror during my past, I would have seen who I thought I was. The little girl that her father abandoned. I didn't know that I was identifying my father's abandonment as my life until God revealed it to me. Remember, I suppress my feelings. One day I was lying in bed, but I wasn't asleep. God began to flashback my life back to the day it all started. I believe I was around 8, 9, or maybe ten years old. My mentor said my ministry began at the age of ten. God gave me a vision; I was in the home I was raised in, standing in the basement on the side of the steps by the telephone. The telephone was significant because I was standing there staring at the phone. God allowed me to hear the exact, relevant thoughts that were going through my mind as I was looking at the phone. I thought about why my father hasn't responded to my letter. He hadn't called me or wrote me back. Before that event, I had written my father a letter. I can't remember everything that I wrote. I only remembered what God deemed was important.

Nonetheless, my mother and father had a falling out, which caused them to break up. I asked my mother his address so I could write to him. She gave me the address or what she thought was his address. I remember asking him why he hadn't reached out to my sisters and me. I went on to say that we didn't have anything to do with him and my mother's relationship. Why did he leave us? I asked him to make sure he called us or wrote me back.

Consequently, when God showed me an image of myself standing there in that basement looking at that phone, with those thoughts running through my mind. That's the day I lost all hope and became extraordinarily disappointed and angry. My self-worth, love, and identity were drowning in pain. I was in so much pain that I never cried until I had my first child. God used her birth to break down some of the callousness that had formed in my heart. As a result, I became a cry baby. I guess I was releasing all the tears I suppressed throughout the years. What I realized then and the revelation I now have are, the tears gave me relief. The role of my biological father was to be an introduction to my Heavenly Father. It was his job to display God's personality, character, and love; that's what I was yearning for, the love of God. It's an unexplained emptiness that you don't realize you have until the void filled if that makes sense. However, after that, I encounter the journey to my identity, healing, and restoration began. Who am I?

- I am a Child of God

Where am I from?

The only one who can answer that question is the one who created us. This answer is in the Book of Genesis. We were just a mere thought and plan that God brought to fruition to fulfill His purpose.

Genesis 1:26-27 (KJV)

"And God said, Let us make man in our image, after our likeness: and let them have dominion over the fish of the sea, and over the fowl of the air, and over the cattle, and over all the earth, and over every creeping thing that creepeth upon the earth. So God created man in His own image, in the image of God created he him; male and female created he them."

Naturally, we are born from our parents. However, the reality is we come from the image of God. No man can take the credit for our existence. We are here as we discussed earlier because God purposed us here. As it relates to the beginning of creation, God formed the woman of the rib of a man.

Genesis 2:21-23 (KJV)

"And The Lord God caused a deep sleep to fall upon Adam, and he slept: and He took one of His ribs, and closed up the flesh instead thereof; And the rib, which the Lord had taken from man, made

He a woman, and brought her unto the man. And Adam said, this is now bone of my bones, and flesh of my flesh: she shall be called woman, because she was taken out of man."

Man's history, as it relates to the beginning of creation, God formed him from the dust of the earth.

Genesis 2:7 (KJV)

"And the Lord God formed man of the dust of the ground and breathed into his nostrils the breath of life; and man became a living soul."

It goes a little deeper than what we see with our natural eyes. God did take the rib from man and form woman and used the dust to form man. However, before creation took place, they both were with God.

Jeremiah 1:5 (KJV)

"Before I formed thee in the belly, I knew thee; and before thou camest forth out of the womb I sanctified thee, and I ordained thee a prophet unto the nations."

What is man? The physical design of our Heavenly Father. In so much that He called us both man. God in His awesomeness has ways that are past figuring out. Miraculously, He used a different method when He created the woman, still in His image.

Genesis 5:1-2 (KJV)

"This is the book of the generations of Adam. In the day that God created man, in the likeness of God made he him. Male and female created he them; and blessed them and called their name Adam, in the day when they were created."

After the first creation, God intended that humans possess the likeness and the image of Him. Consequently, because of man's disobedience when they ate of the fruit, man is now born in sin and shaped in iniquity, which is the image and likeness of Satan. Now humanity must be transformed back into the image of God through His Son,

Jesus Christ, and the Holy Spirit (*See 1 John 4:10.*) For example, I saw the movie, "The Lion King" with my family; I was convinced it was an illustrated sermon. We spoke in the introduction about the protagonist, which is the hero. And the antagonist who is the villain in any script. In the movie, Simba and his father were the protagonists. And Mufasa's brother Scar was the antagonist. Scar was jealous of Mufasa and Simba because he felt like he should be king. Scar began to plot against Mufasa with Mufasa's enemy. He knew Mufasa would do anything to protect his son. Scar convinced Simba to go with him just to get him caught in a stampede, which led to his father's death while trying to save him.

Consequently, his plan worked, he killed his brother. Subsequently, he manipulated Simba into believing it was his fault that his father had died and persuaded him to leave. Simba left hurt, depressed, and ashamed, never wanting to return. As a result, Scar became king. So, Simba was willing to give up his birthright as king; he didn't want any part of it because he was discouraged. He found a new family and a new way of life and became quite comfortable in his newly discovered identity. Until a childhood friend found him and told him, they were in trouble because of Scar, and they needed his help. Simba rejects her, then Rafiki (a mandrill) who I deemed a prophet came and said: "You need to return home, that is what your father would've wanted, you are the king!"

Simba said: "I can't do this without my father. He goes on to say I AM NOT MY FATHER!" Rafiki tells Simba his father was not dead, Simba says he's not dead? Rafiki replies; no, follow me. Rafiki takes Simba through the bushes and trees, and they arrived at this river. Then he tells him to look, "He's right here!" "Where is he? I can't see him," says Simba. Rafiki tells him to look down in the river; he's right here. Simba says in distress, I don't see him. However, Rafiki asked him to look one more time. Simba looks again, and he sees the image of his father.

Rafiki says to him, Mufasa is not dead, because he lives in you. This analogy is another example of someone knowing their name and not knowing who they are. Also, because Simba didn't know who he was, he was willing to settle for being less than he was purposed to become. It was his inheritance! Simba's birthright was to be king, the potential to be king was in him all the time, but he lacked the confidence because he believed what the enemy (Scar) said about him. Once Rafiki uncovered that which was buried in Simba's heart and reminded him who he was, Simba was able to walk in his authority and TRUE identity: a king! He went back, but not without a fight, and took back what was rightfully his, the kingdom!

I said all that to say, God's image doesn't have a race, color, or culture; our God is love. We can find God anywhere; in the grocery store, department store, at the airport. Wherever we go in the world because when you are looking at God's children, you're looking at the likeness and image of God. The enemy's intention was for us to lose or remain ignorant of our TRUE identity. Also, to manipulate us into believing our current situation defines our identity. As we discussed earlier, Naomi changing her name to Mara. Some people are so comfortable in their immediate condition when they look in the mirror; they see depression, abandonment, a female dog, an alcoholic, etc. And have allowed these conditions to take ownership of their life. Your situation is not who you are, no matter what you see on the outside! It's what's on the inside that matters. We have the beauty, love, and the authority of God dwelling in us and around us, through His children. Where am I from?

- God, His Image and His likeness

1 John 4:13 NIV

"We know that we live in Him and He in us because He has given us of His Spirit."

Why Am I Here?

Why were we created? God's intentions in creating the woman are also in the Book of Genesis. When God created man, God said it was not good for man to be alone. One of the definitions of alone is: "Being without another's help or participation; single-handed, in the company of no one else." I believe this reveals the reason: God wasn't thinking about Adam being lonely. God's specific words were: "I will make Him a helpmeet." God didn't say I will make him a companion so that he won't be lonely, or a sex partner to fulfill his sexual needs. He said, a helper (worker). Helpmeet the Hebrew translation means: "To aid, assist." In other words, God created a woman to assist the man with his responsibility.

Dr. Myles Munroe says: "He gave Adam work before He gave him a wife."

1 Corinthians 11:8-9 (NIV)

"For man did not come from woman, but woman from man; neither was man created for woman, but woman for man."

In the beginning, before corruption, the position of a helper was the woman's divine nature, just as it was man's divine nature to lead. However, because the woman usurped her authority, this changed the dynamic of her original purpose.

Genesis 2:18 (NIV)

"The Lord God said, it is not good for man to be alone. I will make a helper suitable for him."

Some women despise the position of helpmeet. One reason for this is because those women want to lead and not follow. Another reason is submission. Some women have a problem submitting to authority. Truthfully, nothing great has ever been accomplished without helpers. The Helper is a powerful and much-needed position. God Himself established it when He created us. One of the most significant accomplishments is humankind; the man needed help to conceive humanity (procreation.)

Genesis 1:28 (NIV)

"God blessed them and said to them, Be fruitful and increase in number; fill the earth and subdue it. Rule over the fish of the sea and the birds of the air and over every living creature that moves on the ground."

Don't let the title fool you. You're created to rule. Being a helper is indeed a leadership position as well. For example, let's use the company, Walmart. Walmart could not function as a department store and a billion-dollar company without helpers. The owner of Walmart had a vision that he was going to open Walmart stores all around the world. For him to accomplish his vision and for it to be successful, he needed managers (helpers). A manager controls the activities, growth, and development of the business. Subsequently, a business' success is going to depend on how the business is managed. The level of management needed is contingent on the size of the company, capacity of people, and the responsibilities. Walmart is not a billion-dollar franchise because of its name. Walmart is a billion-dollar franchise because of it being a well-organized enterprise. We are also this (helpers) to our households, and our household's success is going to depend on how well we manage it. Our husband needs us to help accomplish his vision for his family and career. We're either going to build it up or tear it down. Most women would like a Godly accomplished man. However, can't manage themselves and $1000 of their own. God used the same concept with our households: an organized structure with each person in their rightful position. Why am I here?

- For Divine Purpose

- Help Meet

- Be Fruitful/Productive

- Increase in Numbers

- Rule

- For Mankind

What Can I Do?

This question deals with our potential. Dr. Myles Munroe says, "Potential is the inherited ability to fulfill a purpose."

It also means having or showing the capacity to become or develop into something in the future. We all have our talents and gifts; see *Ephesians 4:6-8*. We have the potential to do a lot of things, but some are gifted at some things than others. However, when God created the woman, He gave her the potential to execute everything He purposed for her to do in this world. As it relates to relationships, every woman has the potential to be a helpmeet, be fruitful and multiply, increase in numbers, and rule. However, those things that were once natural to us now must be taught *see Titus 2:3-5*. Moreover, because Eve wasn't a good manager, she stepped out of her position and catastrophically changed the dynamic of her original purpose. Consequently, it affected humanity as a whole, and Adam, unfortunately, allowed it. Everyone that desires marriage is not marriage material. However, take courage. You can be developed into becoming marriage material because all women have the potential to be a purposeful wife.

1 Timothy 4:7 (NIV)

"Have nothing to do with godless myths and old wives' tales, rather, train yourself to be godly."

Stay away from the old wayward wives' tales that teach practical tactics on how to keep a man. Toss them out and allow God to train you according to His Word and principles, not the world's image. There is a difference between a woman in the world and a woman of the world. What does a woman in the world represent? The image of God: she's the beauty of holiness. She is the female image of God and wisdom. Just as God delivered Eve to Adam, He will render you to your husband. Once He makes and molds you to be the wife, you are to be, for your husband, not a boyfriend. Every man doesn't require the same thing. Every man has their likes and dislikes. What may work for one man may not work for another. That's when the Wisdom of God and resilience comes in. God said I would make a woman suitable for him. The keywords are "for him," God gives us the wisdom to help him, not to help every Tom and Harry. That word "suitable" means right or appropriate for a particular and specific person. The term "particular" means to single out an individual. Individual means: "Designed for use by one person." That may be one of the reasons why our past relationships didn't work because we weren't the one that held the potential wisdom to help him. These results weren't because we weren't good women; it's because we weren't designed to be with them in the first place. The right woman has the potential to take a dead-beat irresponsible man, and help transition him into a full-fledged, responsible man. That is what defines a real man and the head of the household. Character, sensitivity to the needs of his family, and taking care of his responsibilities. When I came to understand this revelation, it helped me to forgive the men of my past relationships. And release them to their wives, allowing God to prepare me for my purposeful husband. What can I do?

- What God gave me the potential to do, fulfill the purpose

Where are you going, your destination?

Psalm 23 NIV

"The Lord is my Shepard, I shall not be in want, He makes me lie down in the green pasture, he leads me beside quiet waters, He restores my soul HE GUIDES ME IN PATHS OF RIGHTEOUSNESS FOR HIS NAME'S SAKE. Even though I walk through the valley of the shadow of death, I will fear no evil, for you are with me; your rod and your staff, they comfort me."

One morning I was getting prepared for prayer service, and this dropped in my spirit; we live in a world of the unknown, and God is trying to show us how to live in it. How do we live in a world of the unknown? By having Faith in God. We don't know what will happen in the next second, minute, or hour. If we knew the answer to everything, we wouldn't rely on God. If we knew, we would avoid adversity, and the life lessons needed to add value to our lives and purpose. The significance of our journey as believers is our faith walk, believing in the unseen (God). The bible declares the just shall live by faith (we live by the unseen). It also states we walk by faith (we walk by the unseen) and not by sight. Besides, through faith, we will see the promises of God manifest. It is by faith in God we will reach our destinations.

My mother raised us in the church, and because my mother had the character of: "Joe Jackson," we were forced to go to church. It wasn't an option like these children today. Because of her forcing us and what I saw and experienced in the church, I rebelled. Unfortunately, at church is where I first experienced what is called a "French kiss." It was NOT consensual. He grabbed me and forced his tongue down my throat. It made me feel some type of way that I couldn't explain at the time, I know now I felt violated, but I never told my mother. In those days, we thought a kiss would make us pregnant. I believe I was around 12 or 13, and the perpetrator so happened to be the pastor's son. It was in the church where I saw homosexuality, infidelity, and preachers giving out lottery numbers, etc., men preying on young girls waiting on the opportunity to get with them. I knew as a child; this behavior wasn't right. When I was allowed to make my own decision on whether I wanted to go or not, I stop going. Some people complain about experiencing church hurt; I was "church confused" if that makes sense. However, I was out there in the street, in my teens partying, just being a teenager. Subsequently, because of my background, I had morals, I wouldn't do some of the things my friends would do. I was always the designated driver. It wasn't until I was grown and had kids of my own; God led me to go back to a church building. However, before my return, I had my relationship with God. I would fast and pray Saturday was the day I set aside to fast; subsequently, I would be working on that day. Saturday was the busiest day for a hairstylist. Nonetheless, when it was time for me to pray, I would stop what I was doing and go into the bathroom and pray. At that time, we had a pastor's wife that would come to the shop to get her hair done. At first, she was the other stylist's client. The stylist would often be late, so either I or someone I designated would prep her. It happened one too many times, and she, as a consequence, became my client. It wasn't by mistake that she became my client; it was by divine appointment. God had sent the church to me, and I would look forward to her coming into the shop. Our conversation would bring life to me because we centered it on God. What I loved and admired about her is she didn't try to get me to attend her church. Just as important, we became good friends. Two things we had in common conversing about God and shopping! One day the subject came up about tithing, she asked me was I tithing. I wasn't because I didn't belong to a church. She went in-depth on how important it was to tithe. That was one of the things I was missing. I knew God sent her to instruct me on the importance of tithing. After our conversation, I started giving her my tithes. My business began to prosper tremendously. The place where I was leasing began to have problems, and I relocated to a bigger space where I was able to have more stations and stylists. During this time, I was in an ungodly relationship with my sons' father. We were on the verge of breaking up, and God exposed him. I found out he was sleeping with one of the stylists and several other women. Nonetheless, when I moved, it was next to a barbershop, I didn't know I was moving next door to my soon to be husband (on the rebound.) The thing that intrigued me about him, he seemed to be knowledgeable in God's Word. One day we were at dinner, and the conversation came up about tithes. He told me that we didn't have to give tithes anymore because its under the Levitical Law. I asked First Lady about it being done away with; she said tithes are giving by faith, before the law. However, like a nut, I eventually listened to him. And my business began to suffer and my finances from it. I only had enough money to pay my rent. Where is my money going? Then one day, this is what got me. I was sitting in the salon, my daughter and I were hungry. We were waiting for him to get something to eat. He left for a moment, that same guy that told me to stop giving my tithes. He left the shop and went to Taco Bell. He returned, eating while my daughter and I were hungry! He hadn't asked if we wanted anything and didn't offer us anything. I couldn't believe how selfish he was! I felt like a penny; I heard God's voice: "This is what happens when you put your trust in man over Me!" No sooner than I went back to work and made my first dollars, I took out my tithes, and God shifted not having enough, to more than enough! I lost confidence in him, who is now my ex-husband, and began to study The Word for myself! He saw the immediate turnaround, that's why no one can convince me not to tithe! I faithfully tithe. Why am I telling you this story? I didn't know myself at first why God led me to tell this one. I believe because every step I took good, bad, or indifferent, He allowed it; it's a part of my faith journey. I also realized you could be going in the right direction, and the enemy will send someone to sabotage your purpose. This episode prepared me for the next level of faith, my future, and my next experience. The Lord told me to start tithing my child's support. I didn't know why, but I was obedient. Every service I went to for about two weeks straight, the minister was preaching on standing through trials! A few days later, all hell broke loose between my ex-husband and me; I had to vacate my house. Then the reason why was made plain it was because I was about to lose my house, my hair salon, and my clients, the only financial means I was going to have was my child support. God was preparing me through the message to stand. Stand on His Word! There's a scripture in the Book of Proverbs that says:

Proverbs 20:24 (KJV)

"Man's goings are of the Lord; how can a man then understand his own way."

I was homeless for one day! The brother at the church I had become a member. He knew a person that worked at these apartments. He took me there, I filled out the application, and got approved! She just needed proof of my income. I went to H&R Block to get a copy of my taxes. And when I spoke with the lady, she looked up my file, and she told me you have two years of tax returns sitting here waiting on a signature. I couldn't believe it. Outdone, all I could say was look at God! Stuck at the moment; she said all you need to do is sign these papers to process it. It was 4000.00 and some odd dollars sitting there waiting on me! God ordered my steps. You may not understand the direction your life is going in and why, because it's unknown. God is leading us in the path of (unseen) righteousness for His namesake. However, you need to understand when you are a child of God; every step you take has a purpose. It is divinely designed just for you and for His glory! The places I thought I should've have been, the things I thought I shouldn't have done, even some of the decisions I made, all led me to PURPOSE! The bible says God has prepared a table before me in the presence of my enemies (Psalm 23.) I desire my table; not anyone else's, because I don't know what they have to endure for their table. I felt like I barely survived mine. Know this one thing for sure, God is not going to put any more on you than you can bear, and you will understand it better when it manifest. I encourage you to have faith in the steps God has prepared for you. If anything, it will lead you to your final destination: eternal life, through Jesus Christ if we continue to believe. Now walk it out with no regrets, no guilt, and no shame, because the best is yet to come. Where am I going?

- In the steps, God planned for me for His namesake by faith

Psalm 37:23 (KJV)

"The steps of a good man are ordered by the Lord: and he delighteth in his way."

CHAPTER 6

DELIVER US FROM EVE: SHE REALLY HAS A HOLD ON US

The events in the Book of Genesis are incredibly relevant to our modern-day society. It also is the very reason why there is turmoil among humanity. From corruption to gender identity issues, etc., just from the simple act of disobeying one single command! Disobedience has consequences; one act can change our whole personal world and those connected to us. Mother Eve was responsible for this disruption. When God gave the command to Adam, Eve didn't exist. However, in her conversation with the serpent, in his attempt to try to persuade her. To eat of the fruit of the tree, her fate (and Adam's) was in jeopardy. She said to him, "God said," what that tells us is Adam told Eve what God had instructed. He said NOT to eat the fruit from the tree in the middle of the garden. She quoted him verbatim. She couldn't use the excuse; she didn't know, because she spoke it out of her mouth. That's when she became accountable.

Nevertheless, Adam was equally responsible as well. He chose to listen to Eve rather than God! When Eve decided to have a dialogue with the serpent, the serpent gained influence over her. (*See Genesis 2:3, 4, 5*) However, by Eve entertaining the words of the enemy, her mind, emotions, heart, and curiosity became open to other possibilities. She began looking at the tree in a different light. Satan gained access, and through his enticement and manipulation, she began having sensual, unnatural desires that, at first, she didn't have. For example, when a man entices a woman to have sexual relations with him even after she tells him no, does he give up? No, he doesn't give up, he keeps on pursuing her. He does whatever it takes, whispering seductive words in her ear, touching, feeling trying to convince her otherwise. As he wakes up those sexual emotions, her mind is saying no, but her body and emotions begin to speak for her. Before she knows it, it's on; as a result, like Satan, he is satisfied because he has accomplished his goal. The devil has no new tricks! He used the same tactic than that he uses today: Lies and Deception! He seeks out those who are emotionally vulnerable and sets them up for the kill! If the truth is told, many of us have fallen prey to his devices at one time or another.

Genesis 3:6 (NIV)

"When the woman saw that the fruit of the tree was good for food and pleasing to the eye, and also desirable for gaining wisdom, she took some and ate it. She also gave some to her husband, who was with her, and he ate it."

Three attributes Eve possessed from her conversation with the serpent:

1. She saw: The Lust of the Eye

2. Pleasing to the eye: Lust of the Flesh

3. Desirable for Gain wisdom: The Pride of Life

These three attributes are of the world, and she initiated by disobeying the Word of *God (See 1 John 2:16.)* They have become a character trait and a stronghold for humankind. Eve wanted to be wise as God, and that came from the spirit of Satan. He got kicked out (of Heaven) because he wanted to be above God. As a result of her partaking of the fruit, Satan's spirit overtook Eve. She disrespected her husband's authority as Satan disrespected God's power.

Romans 13:1-2 (NIV)

"Everyone must submit himself to the governing authorities, for there is no authority except that which God has established. The authorities that exist have been established by God. Consequently, he who rebels against the authority is rebelling against what God has instituted, and those who do so will bring judgement on themselves."

The part the serpent left out: THE CONSEQUENCES! God gave the consequences to Adam: "If you eat, you will surely die." Through disobedience, now Eve's influence had changed from what God had said to what the serpent was saying!

Romans 8:4 (NIV)

"In order that the righteous requirements of the law might be fully met in us, who do not live according to the sinful nature but according to the Spirit."

Eve repeated the cycle! The same temptation the serpent used against her, she brought before Adam and enticed him to eat. The snake needed a vessel to execute his plan on the earth. He required both the man and the woman to bring it to completion.

James 1:13-15 (NIV)

"When tempted, no one should say, 'God is tempting me.' For God cannot be tempted by evil, nor does He tempt anyone; but each one is tempted when, by his own evil desire, he is dragged away and enticed. Then, after desire has conceived, it gives birth to sin; and sin, when it is full-grown, gives birth to death."

Duly note, we can't conquer what we don't understand. My purpose for speaking on this subject is three things: One perspective is to reveal why God created the woman. So that she can walk in her full power and authority, taking her rightful place in the Kingdom, household, and in the earth. Two, I want to show you the effects it had on the Family structure when a husband and a wife are not functioning in their God-given positions. Three, to expose the spirit of Eve and break its generational curse. It's so crucial for the future generation to know this! Ultimately, as a result of what she did, the roles have been reversed. The Family structure is dysfunctional and out of its original order, affecting humanity negatively.

Genesis 3:17 (NIV)

"To Adam, he said, 'Because you listened to your wife and ate from the tree about which I commanded you, you must not eat of it,' Cursed is the ground because of you; through painful toil you will eat of it all the days of your life."

There are two phrases we MUST focus on:

1. "Because you Listened to Your Wife."

2. "Cursed is the Ground Because of You."

Just as important, Adam was established by God as the head of the family. His disobedience caused man's malfunctioning state today because he allowed Eve to lead. He permitted Satan and Eve to undermine his authority. However, because Adam listened to his wife over what God instructed, a curse was given. God instituted marriage; if we enter into the institution of marriage, not knowing or taking our rightful position, the marriage is out of Divine Order. As a result, women are running the household, functioning in the headship position, cowering down the husband. Hence, enabling him, as Eve did, instead of helping him, she becomes a hindrance. A stumbling block, as we discussed earlier. When we take authority over the man, the results are still the same; a dysfunctional household.

The only person that is feeling satisfied is the woman, and her alters ego. However, when the woman is in her rightful position as his help, she is powerful, the order is established, and the blessings can flow. Women: are you aware that some of his greatest achievements in life he won't achieve until he connects with you? That's how significant you are to his purpose? *(see Chapter 13: A Man of Godly Character is Hard to Find)* As we discussed earlier, the importance of us being with the right one. We are the favor if we are in alignment with the Kingdom of God. However, joined to the wrong man can result in them abusing our support because they don't understand who we are to them. As a result, we become the enemy.

Let's go a little deeper about Eve; we know she obtained another nature through disobedience. Did you know that disobedience is also a form of witchcraft (*See: 1 Samuel 15:23*) Three of the characteristics disobedience produced are: **Control, Manipulation, and Seduction.** We inherited this from Eve, the mother of all living things. Additionally, we have the power through our sexuality to use it for evil or good. Some women have full knowledge of the power they possess to seduce men (evil intentions). For some marriages, the foundation is built entirely on sex. When you use sex to entrap a husband, that's a form of witchcraft. The intent isn't pure, that's using sex as a negative influence, and it's ungodly. In God's original creative plan for man, sexual intercourse was a positive concept. Remember, it's all about our motives. Also, marriages based on the sexual drive alone, don't usually last long, because the only thing they have in common is sex. One of them is going to desire more than a sexual partner in the marriage eventually. You can get sex anywhere. You need stability, substance, and growth, among other vital things. Most importantly, the union needs a solid foundation: LOVE.

"Sex is the cherry on top, not the glue that holds it together!"

TWO TYPES OF WOMEN

Two types of women established as the fallout of Eve's disobedience. One influenced by sin; she is WAYWARD, and God controls the other; she is VIRTUOUS! When God created the woman, he built her with

His nature. Unfortunately, the character we inherited due to the Fall of Man becomes both good and evil. Two opposing powers are called dualism. When we become conscious of these two rival powers, we must choose a side. God is against dualism (wavering). He says in the Book of Revelation, there is no in-between which He calls "lukewarm," it's also referred to as: "straddling the fence." Either we are going to be hot or cold, or He will spit us out of his mouth (See Revelation 3:15-17.), in other words, a person in the Church and the World. Gospel Recording Artist, Jonathan Reynolds has a song entitled: "No Gray" There's a portion in his lyrics that says: "We can't have our cake and eat it too. We got to be white or black; there are no grey areas." Either we are going to be a virtuous woman or a wayward woman. We can't be both, that's the premise of this subject. Let's make a clear distinction as it relates to them both. Let's deal with the spirit, principles, and attributes of the wayward woman first. When God takes us through our healing process, he exposes us. He doesn't unmask us with evil intentions to judge or ridicule us. He does it to get to the root for healing purposes, and more importantly, because He loves us. It's easier to point out someone else's imperfections than to face our ugly truth! Knowing the truth will make you free (*See: John 3:32.*) God exposed me; I had some nasty ungodly ways. He used this man I worked with to expose the root of my issue. What I disclosed in an earlier chapter: abandonment. He asked me a question; to me, it was out of the blue! However, it wasn't, it came through his observation of me, and he was God sent. He asked me who raised me? I gave him a strange, disturbing look. He asked, "Was my father in the home?" I said, why? "Because you have a problem with male authority." I said, "How have you came to that conclusion?" He said, "Your tone and attitude change when a male gives you orders, verses a woman." I didn't go off on him, which would have been my usual reaction. I couldn't respond because something in me knew he was right. Being raised by my mother, her tone wouldn't offend me.

On the contrary, if it were a man, I would immediately get an attitude. I was married to my first husband at the time when my coworker revealed this to me. I can admit I was very disrespectful during that time in my life. Before my marriage, I had no remorse for men. Hurt people hurt other people; I firmly believe this to be true!

Studies show that men think about sex every seven seconds. Sex is usually their motivation when they first meet a woman. Out of curiosity, I asked one of my coworkers was this true. He said, "Yes." I also asked him, "What's on your mind when you first meet a woman?" He answered, "Can I get it?" How I'm going to get it? What must I do to get it? I was already aware of this, and this is what I used in the past to my advantage. I was going to get them before they were going to get me. I knew the 90-day rule well before Entertainer/Comedian, Mr. Steve Harvey revealed it in his book; "Act like a Woman, Think Like a Man" I used the man's mentality (his way of thinking) against him. With no intention of getting with them sexually, just to use them for whatever I could. When it was over, they didn't know if I was a man or a woman. They had no sexual knowledge of me. My mother told me if I didn't stop, it would be the death of me. It was by the grace of God I survived that period in my life. Believe you me; I got it back in a different way. One thing is for sure we are going to reap what we sow, playing those types of games can backfire! Nonetheless, I thought my first husband was getting the best part of me. When I decided to give a real relationship a chance and do the honorable thing, to settle down and get married. However, because I didn't respect men, it became a significant problem in my marriage. Every man was guilty in my eyes because of the absence of my father. Consequently, all my relationships with men at that point were unhealthy. I was still angry. I just used a different tactic to display it as a wife.

1 Corinthians 7:4-5 (NIV)

"The wife's body does not belong to her alone but also to her husband. In the same way, the husband's body does not belong to him alone but also to his wife. Do not deprive each other except by mutual consent and for a time, so that you may devote yourselves

to prayer. Then come together again so that Satan will not tempt you because of your lack of self-control.

For example, when we use our bodies to control our husbands. By using sex to punish him and bring him under subjection and being spiteful and depriving him because you're mad or to get what you want. Or, in my case, having no respect for them in the first place. In any case, that's also using your goods for evil. To control and manipulate your husband, which is a form of witchcraft.

I'VE BEEN THERE, done that, out of ignorance, and being in a loveless marriage. On some occasions, I didn't have the desire for sexual relations, and to be honest; I just didn't feel like faking it. However, the Bible tells us to give no place to the devil. When we are depriving our partner, we're opening ourselves and him to temptation. Men are not the only ones that are harlots and play mind games. Women are very capable of it as well. I believe women do it better.

WAYWARD WOMAN

Type One:

Wayward: Difficult to control or predict because of unusual or perverse behavior. Headstrong, obstinate, disobedient, perverse, contrary, insubordinate, undisciplined, rebellious, defiant, uncooperative, unruly, wild, unmanageable, erratic, difficult, impossible.

Some ladies are genuinely oblivious to the fact that there are two types of women. I was one of them. It was beyond my rationalization and consciousness. No one taught me; I did what I thought came naturally to me. Besides, just because we are accustomed to doing things one way doesn't mean it is necessarily right. It's equally as important to know if we remain silent, we will lose the quality, importance, and value of a woman throughout this generation. Unconsciously, we are losing this generation to a standard through social media, reality TV, and other misleading, deceptive devices. Unfortunately, some women thrive off this behavior because they like the result and the attention they receive. Sadly, they are teaching other women their craft. However, there is excellent news; even they can become a virtuous woman through God's grace. There is nothing new under the sun. God reveals this type of woman throughout the Bible. Allow me to show you, according to His Word, just how dangerous she can be!

"Overcoming negative behavior is a challenge!" – Les Brown

Characteristics of a Wayward Woman:

• Adulteress: a woman who commits adultery.

Proverbs 7:19-27 (NIV)

"My husband is not at home; he has gone on a long journey. He took his purse filled with money and will not be home till full moon. With persuasive words she led him astray; she seduced him with her smooth talk. All at once he followed her like an ox going to the slaughter, like a deer stepping into a noose till an arrow pierces his liver, like a bird darting into a snare, little knowing it will cost him his life. Now then, my sons, listen to me; pay attention to what I say. Do not let your heart turn to her ways or stray into her paths. Many are the victims she has brought down; her slain are a mighty throng. Her house is a highway to the grave, leading down to the chambers of death."

• Prostitute: A person who misuses their talents or who sacrifices their self-respect for the sake of personal or financial gain. Prostitution is not limited to the street corner or multiple partners; all it takes is one.

Proverbs 23:26-28 (NIV)

"My son, give me your heart and let your eyes delight in my ways, for a prostitute woman is a deep pit and a wayward wife is a

narrow well. Like a bandit, she lies in wait and multiplies the unfaithful among men."

• Immoral: Not conforming to accepted standards of morality. Unethical, bad, wrongful, wicked, evil, unprincipled, dishonorable, dishonest, corrupt, devious, vile, etc.,

Proverbs 6:23-26 (NIV)

"For these commands are a lamp, this teaching is a light, and the corrections of discipline are the way of life, keeping you from the immoral woman, from the smooth tongue of the wayward wife. Do not lust in your heart after her beauty or let her captivate you with her eyes, for the prostitute reduces you to a loaf of bread, and the adulteress preys upon your very life."

Wayward Women in the Bible and their Attributes:

Foreign Women (1 Kings Chapter 11)

• Manipulative: Characterized by unethical control of a situation or person.

The best and for sure way to sabotage a man, send a wayward woman. Especially a man with lust issues like King Solomon. King Solomon loved many women. He had 700 hundred wives and 300 concubines. The Bible says his wives led him astray. God told Solomon not to intermarry with these (wayward type) foreign women because they were going to turn his heart after other gods. In the Old Testament, when a couple married, they had sexual intercourse, the term they would use is: "Lay with or knew them." It hasn't changed, it's the same today. When you have sex with another person, you become one. It is my personal belief that's what happened in the Garden of Eden with Adam and Eve. If a conversation can have those persuasive powers. How much more power will the act of sex?

1 Corinthians 6:15-17 (NIV)

"Do you know that your bodies are members of Christ himself? Shall I then take the members of Christ and unite them with a prostitute? Never! Do you not know that he who unites himself with a prostitute is one with her in body? For it is said, the two become one flesh. But he who unites himself with the Lord is one with him in spirit."

God's intention for sex was to be a positive emotion exclusively. However, when the Fall of Man occurred, that's when another passion arose, adding the negative and its consequences. It doesn't eliminate what God initially established. You will find it in the Old Testament and confirmed in the New Testament as well. In Genesis 2:24, when He first created man, as well as the scripture above. What validates one's marriage is sex. Marriage is not just standing in front of a Justice of the Peace or Minister reciting your vows. One is officially married once they have sex; the term is consummating your marriage.

Consummate: make a marriage or relationship complete by having sexual intercourse.

Without sex, the marriage is null and void having no legal force; invalid and of no consequences, effects, or value, it's insignificant. We are of spirit, body, and soul. Consequently, this act used negatively is a violation of the body. It creates what's called soul ties and strongholds. Furthermore, if we have sex before we walked down the aisle, we have already married them before the spoken vows and the commitment. We have already broken the Laws of God through fornication and sexual immorality, making the beautiful covenant of marriage created by God desecrated rather than consecrated. As a result, it's an ungodly marriage or union, but it's still a marriage. Perhaps this is new to some of you, so let's take it a little further, including a discussion about multiple partners. Do you know how a sexual disease is transmitted? From one sexual partner to another. When you have sex with someone that has numerous sex partners, you're having sex with everyone that your partner has had sexual relations. It works the same way with the body. Everyone the both of you has had sex with, have become one with your body. You are transmitting unfamiliar spirits unconsciously. More importantly, you may not know, but those spirits have influence, which you lie down with, you become unintentionally. For example, violation, let say rape, even though it's an involuntary act of rape (which is a negative sex emotion,) doesn't negate the after-effects. In view of it being sexual contact, that person has taken on the characteristics of the perpetrator, involuntarily. Some result in promiscuous behavior. And doing acts outside of your character. Also, outside the nature of God. Or they become the perpetrator, refrain, or all the above. Dr. Myles Monroe said it like this "When certain parts of our bodies are touched, certain enzymes and chemicals that trigger sexual desires release into our system. The more our bodies are stimulated, the more chemicals are released and the greater our sexual desires grows until it becomes a virtually unstoppable flood." Speaking for myself, when I separated from my ex-husband from my second marriage, I was still having sex with him. We were still trying to make our marriage work, my reason I didn't want another failed marriage. However, we were living in different houses. He was always verbally abusive. I would struggle with allowing him to come over, even during sex, I felt empty. God told me to stop having sex with him because through sex; I was enabling him to have power over me. God calls it: "turning your heart." I didn't think anything was wrong with it except for the way he made me feel afterward. I figured he was still my husband, and I wasn't fornicating; technically, I wasn't; emotionally speaking; however, repeatedly violated. I obeyed God and stopped, but I still was dealing with the residual effects. Sex will leave you yearning, attached and desiring your abuser simultaneously! However, the longer I stayed away from him, it began to dissipate. Oh, and another thing I had to stop all conversations. Then I was able to see the relationship for what it was, OVER! His intentions weren't right. Sex is the reason why a woman could be getting the curse word beat out of her and keep going back. It's a powerful draw! If you genuinely want to be delivered from someone, you must stop having sexual intercourse and break all lines of communication with them. Sex is the tie that binds! Seriously, casual sex just isn't casual. It's more to it than just a feeling of pleasure. Nevertheless, King Solomon remained with foreign women. Those women influenced him; as a result, his heart was turned from God to other gods through sexual intercourse. I know he was out of his mind because of lying with those women. If you saw the movie "Get Out," Solomon was in that sunken place. Negative emotional sex will take a person to a sunken place. What made it cynical? The lady's intentions were evil; God knew their hearts; that's why He forbid it. Consequently, because he disobeyed God, he lost his Kingdom, and it affected the livelihood of the people and his children.

1 Corinthians 6:18-20 (NIV)

"Flee from sexual immorality. All other sins a man commits are outside his body, but he who sins sexually sins against his own body. Do you not know that your body is a temple of the Holy Spirit, who is in you, whom you have received from God? You are not your own; you were bought at a price. Therefore honor God with your body."

Jezebel (1 Kings 21:7)

Controlling: The power to influence or direct people's behavior or the course of events.

Anyone within the church syndicate has heard of the spirit of Jezebel. A Jezebel spirit can ruin a church and a household. Jezebel's husband was King Ahab. Take note that these were men of influence, holding influential positions. He also married outside the Will of God to a woman who incited him to abandon the worship of Yahweh. Additionally, she persecuted the prophets of God. King Ahab married the daughter of the King of Sidonia, worshipers of Baal. In the sight of God, Ahab did more evil than any other ruler because he married (wayward type) Jezebel. What provoked God besides marrying someone OUTSIDE HIS WILL was what he allowed her to do on his behalf. King Ahab coveted another man's property. The man wouldn't sell his property because He had inherited this vineyard from his father. The king went home angry and depressed, his wife asked him what was wrong, he explained to her what happened, and she went off. I guess she believed she was acting in his best interest. She demanded him to get up and eat! She took control of the situation. She told Ahab is this how a king behaves, questioning his status and authority as king. She was about to show him how to do it. She was determined to get the property for him! She caused Naboth to face scrutiny. She ordered the execution of Naboth on her husbands' behalf. She wrote a letter to the elders and the nobles and signed her husband's name. In the letter, she called a fast, she had two scoundrels set opposite sides of him and testify against him, saying Naboth cursed God and the King. Then she requested that he be taken outside and stoned. They carried out the plan and killed him because they believed the request came from the king. She (Jezebel) exerted drastic measures. Consequently, because King Ahab allowed Jezebel to control the situation, usurping his authority, God dealt with them severely. Sound familiar? The same scenario from the Garden of Eden! Because he listened to the woman, a curse was placed on his entire family! King Ahab had no remorse for what they did, he believed, and she made him think he was entitled because he was king. That's why it's essential to know and follow suit in your proper role within the family. Just as important, marrying someone in the will of God. Instead of her being a blessing, she became a liability.

1 Kings 21:17-21 (NIV)

"Then the word of the Lord came to Elijah the Tishbite: Go down to meet Ahab king of Israel, who rules in Samaria. He is now in Naboth's vineyard, where he has gone to take possession of it. Say to him, 'This is what the Lord says: Have you not murdered a man and seized his property?' Then say to him, 'This is what the Lord says: In the place where dogs licked up Naboth's blood, dogs, will lick up your blood yes, yours!' "Ahab said to Elijah, "So you have found me, my enemy!" "I have found you," he answered, "because you have sold yourself to do evil in the eyes of the Lord. I am going

to bring disaster on you. I will consume your descendants and cut off from Ahab every last male in Israel slave or free."

Jezebel's Punishment:

1 Kings 21:23 (NIV)

"And also concerning Jezebel the Lord says: 'Dogs will devour Jezebel by the wall of Jezreel.' "

1 Kings 21:25-26 (NIV)

"There was never a man like Ahab, who sold himself to do evil in the eyes of the Lord, urged on by Jezebel his wife. He behaved in the vilest manner by going after idols, like the Amorites the Lord drove out before Israel."

Delilah:

Power of persuasive words: Good at persuading someone to do or believe something by reasoning or the use of temptation.

According to the Bible, Sampson loved women. The love he had for one woman named Delilah was going to be the literal death of him. He, like Solomon, also intermarried with foreign women. Sampson was a Nazarite from birth. A Nazarite was consecrated to the service of God under the vow of abstaining from drinking wine or eating unclean things. He was a Man of God with high authority and power. The secret to his power was never to put a razor to his head. On one occasion, the spirit of the Lord came upon him, and he tore a young lion apart with his bare hands. He had mighty strength. The Philistines knew they couldn't defeat Sampson because they tried on many occasions. However, they also found out he had a weakness. He loved Delilah! The Philistines made an offer to her to help them subdue Sampson. As the scripture reveals, she loved money more than she loved him.

Judges 16:4 (NIV)

"**Sometime later, he fell in love with a woman in the valley of**

Sorek whose name was Delilah. The ruler of the Philistines went to her and said, "See if you can lure him into showing you the secrets to his great strength and how we can overpower him so we may tie him up and subdue him. Each one of us will give you eleven hundred shekels of silver."

Driven by the love of money, she began trying to persuade him to release the secret. Delilah tried three times and was unsuccessful. Nevertheless, she didn't give up. She knew this one thing, his love for women was his weakness, and she used it against him.

Judges 16:15-17 (KJV)

"And she said unto him, how canst thou say, I love thee, when thine heart is not with me? Thou hast mocked me these three times, and hast not told me wherein thy great strength lieth. And it came to pass, when she pressed him daily with her words, and urged him, so that his soul was vexed unto death; That he told her all his heart, and said unto her, there hath not come a razor upon mine head; for I have been a Nazarite unto God from my mother's womb: if I be shaven, then my strength will go from me, and I shall become weak, and be like any other man."

She broke him down with her words to the depth of his soul. Also, this a tactic of the enemy. His point of attack is our mind. Additionally, he uses words, our lustful desires, and weaknesses to bring us to our demise. The persuasive devices wayward women use is motivated by what we discussed earlier: The lust of the eye, the lust of the flesh, the pride of life, and the love of the world.

Consequently, as the Bible reveals, she brings her victims down! She turns their hearts! She is a highway to the grave and a chamber of death. Wayward women is a negative influence and have a negative emotional attitude. Additionally, they lead counter-productive unsuccessful, and unfruitful lives. These behaviors, attributes, and principles are inherited from Mother Eve. She established the sinful and disobedient behavior as it relates to the womanhood.

Spirits as they pertain to the Wayward Woman:

• Foreign, Women Sexually Enticing

• Jezebel, Controlling

• Delilah, Seductive Words

These spirits do not have a gender preference (as some may believe) men can possess these spirits as well. The Bible refers to them as: "wicked men." Proverbs tells us how to be saved from the ways of the wicked man, the adulteress, the wayward wife with her seductive words.

Saved Through Wisdom:

Proverbs 2:12-19 (NIV)

"Wisdom will save you from the ways of wicked men, from men whose words are perverse, who leave the straight paths to walk in dark ways, who delight in doing wrong and rejoice in the perverseness of evil, whose paths are crooked and who are devious in their ways. It will save you also from the adulteress, from the wayward wife with her seductive words, who has left the partner of her youth and ignored the covenant she made before God. For her house leads down to death and her paths to the spirits of the dead. None who go to her return or attain the paths of life."

CHAPTER 7

VIRTUOUS WOMAN: TYPE TWO

*V*irtue: Behavior showing high moral standards, chaste, goodness, righteousness, noble, having integrity, dignity, honesty, decency, trustworthiness, respectability, lack of corruption, pureness, having merit.

There are always at least two sides to a story. Can a good person do something bad? Absolutely! Jesus said there is nobody good, but one. Good and evil remains a constant battle with mankind. Apostle Paul said when I try to do good, evil is always present. He was speaking about the battle within himself. We are all capable of doing anything and everything. It's by the grace of God we are restrained from doing some of the bad things we have the potential of doing. That's why it's imperative that the woman understands who she is in God. One of the greatest disadvantages we face is our lack of knowledge of who we really are. We spoke briefly in an early chapter about our identity. Now let's talk about the importance of why it's crucial to know who we are as it relates to us women. Consequently, when we don't know who we are, we are subject to compromise. We will conform to the standard of others, rather than God's, and allow others to influence us with their own carnal desires. Unfortunately, this leads to depression, and I might also add, it is a form of mental illness among other things. Being TOLD who you are and KNOWING who you are two very different things. I've come across many unhappy women due to this dilemma. I can strongly identify with them, as I said earlier, I was once one of them. I was trying to be everything for everyone else and neglecting myself. As a result, I was despising who I allowed myself to become. I could only pretend for a while, the REAL image of who God created me to be was fighting to come out! Fighting to be who God created me to be before the foundation of the world, before I uttered my first words. Before I knew my Mother and my Father's image and their DNA, I had His (God's) image! I needed to be free to be me, to express myself, my feelings, my opinion, my likes and dislikes; without caring what people said or thought about me. Needing no form of validation from other people and more importantly, loving and appreciating myself. This level of freedom we can only have in Jesus Christ! I do understand there are restrictions, rules and regulations, and the Do's and Dont's in life. However, those restrictions when you're a child of God, are mandated by God through His Word, not man. This is one of the reasons you need to have a relationship with God for yourself, to find out your own identity, who you are, whose you are, and what He's requiring of you as a woman. Then we will stop allowing people to keep us in chains. I'm reminded of the song by Gospel Artist, Tasha Cobbs Leonard who sings "Break Every Chain." In order for chains to be broken we must recognize that we are in chains. Women are beautiful in our Godly essence, God created us in a unique way, to be different. Women can be amazing! On the other hand, as we read, some women can be treacherous, haters, backbiters, spiteful, envious, and jealous in our worldly essence. As we discussed previously both abilities reside in us. Unfortunately, women have also grown accustomed to some form of bondage through creation and social traditions; that's why it's not hard for women to conform to man. Also, to confuse love with control, because we are more apt to control. In some countries, religions, and even in the United States of America it is customary for the women to be enslaved to men, some believe it's a way of life. Unfortunately, mothers teach their daughters how to be enslaved, passing restrictive behavior down from generation to generation. Yes, it is said in the Bible the older women are to teach the young. However, a woman can only teach from a perspective of who they are and what they have knowledge of. A bound (wayward) woman can't teach other females how to be free, love, and manage their husband and children in a godly perspective.

Three Categories of Imprisonment:

1. Confined behind Bars

2. Confined in the Mind

3. Confined under the Control of Someone or Something

This is a ploy from the devil to keep us in chains. Additionally, he uses us as he used our foremothers to keep the next generation in chains, it's just a vicious cycle. What some may not know is when the woman is free her children, and her husband will be free. I will show you in the Word of our beautiful God how extraordinary and precious his original creation of the woman is. There is a plethora of benefits attached to be a virtuous (righteous) woman. As one who came from several abusive, unhealthy, and traumatic relationships, let me share with you what's my greatest fulfillment of being a virtuous woman. Above all, the greatest for me is PEACE! This Peace I have, the world didn't give it to me, and the world can't take it away! I can't begin to articulate the consolation God has given me within. However, I can say this, it is worth more than any material possessions or any man sleeping beside me in bed. Peace takes away frustration, disappointments, and anxiety, while you're waiting and relying on God. Peace is something money cannot purchase; or any person on God's green earth can give. A friend of mine describes it like being wrapped in a warm blanket, she said it's just the right temperature. Peace is a byproduct of righteousness that comes from trusting God, it is priceless!

Isaiah 32:17 (NIV)

"The fruit of righteousness will be peace; the effect of righteousness will be quietness and confidence forever."

Proverbs 31 Woman

"Becoming a Proverbs 31 Woman isn't as hard as you think. In fact, Proverbs 31 is not a Checklist or a To Do List. Instead, it's a beautiful representation of what it means to be a virtuous woman."

– A Virtuous Woman

A Proverbs 31 Woman is God's Woman, she is blessed (happy). She is set apart by God. She's the epitome of God's intentions when He created her. Her qualities and attributes are Divine. She leaves something to the imagination, she's a mystery. It's not her outside appearance that makes her valuable, it's what she has on the inside and the unique qualities she exhibits that make her priceless. She loves and reverences the Lord with all her heart, mind, and soul. And she desires to do what is pleasing to Him. She seems surreal, doesn't she? She's not surreal, just rare. Being a virtuous woman doesn't mean you have to be perfect, it's about living a purposeful life. Someone who has many imperfections, however, her Love, Hope and Faith are in the Lord.

"Men themselves have wondered what they see in me. They try so much but they can't touch my inner mystery."

– Maya Angelou

A Virtuous Woman's Attributes

- Faithful to God and Man

- Maternal; She Nurtures and Teaches her Children

- Servant; Serves her Family and Friends

- Stewardship; Spends money wisely
- Industrial; Works willingly with her hands
- Homemaker; Manages her Home
- Beautiful; Inner beauty derived from a Holy Lifestyle
- Wise; She speaks with Wisdom
- Diligent, Completes her tasks
- Helpmeet, Respects and Supports her Husband

Proverbs 12:4 (NIV)

"A wife of noble character is her husband's crown, but a disgraceful wife is like decay in his bones."

KNOWING YOUR WORTH

Depiction Number One:

For me there were three depictions of how I viewed men. They were the depictions of my father. In correspondence with the three stages of my development As a Child, a Woman, and a Virtuous Woman. Now, I have the revelation Paul was speaking about in the Book 1 Corinthians 13:11 through personal experience when he said: "When I was a child I talked like a child, I thought like a child, I reasoned like a child…." When you are a child your mind is not developed to rationalize like an adult. There was a combination of things I didn't know or even thought about before I got married. One were my vows, second marrying in God's Will, and the third my worth. When I got married, I was 22 years old, my ex-husband and I were kids we just wanted to be together forever. We were oblivious about life and what it took to build a future together. As I shared previously, I didn't have an example of a paternal figure growing up in my home. Which impaired me to be able to recognize what was a right and acceptable behavior for a husband. My first husband was extremely controlling, jealous, possessive and an alcoholic from the beginning. Because of my ignorance, I made a commitment to who he was, and he was being himself. For example, when he was still living with his mother and father and I was living at home with my mother, he was possessive even then. He had a job working at a restaurant, before he would go to work, he would pick me up and bring me over his mother's house and I would stay there with his family until he got off work. At that time, I didn't think nothing of it, I was blinded by what I thought was love. He began to start telling me what to wear. I'm thinking that he cared, but it wasn't that he cared, it was his own insecurity he was passing on to me. These are some of the things he did before we got married. I didn't realize at the time that God was revealing this to me because I saw it, but I married him anyway. What I saw and felt was familiar to me, I had seen in my childhood, the limited time my father was in the home. There was always confrontation. I can remember saying to myself as a child in the first grade: "I'm not going to ever marry a drunk." I despised my father for being an alcoholic because every time he came home, he and my mother would get into fights and arguments. That seed was planted in me very early. How ironic, what I despised, I was attracted to! It was FAMILIAR! Nonetheless, after we got married it escalated to where I could and could not go, to who or what I could even look at with my own eyes. This would cause major arguments, and frustration but I made a commitment to it. I didn't like confrontation, there were times I would simply give in and suppress my feelings just to keep the peace. After nine years of suppressing and conforming, the pressure became so overwhelming and I just couldn't take it anymore. I had two daughters I didn't want them to be traumatized like I was. At that point, I asked him would he consider counseling, he refused. Then, I just wanted out. I stopped having sex with him and started disrespecting him with other men I didn't care anymore. In my irony I didn't realize I was disrespecting myself. When we speak about having worth and identity, as a kid those words were foreign to me.

Depiction Number Two:

As a woman only by age not by definition and character, I was still "Chasing Jason" this is a term we used in Michigan. The concept of chasing Jason came from the crack cocaine era of the 1980's. When it's someone's first time hitting the crack pipe, I've been told the initial hit gives them a feeling that is better than an orgasm. No matter how much crack they smoke they can never get that feeling again. That provokes the chase, because they are always in search of that feeling that they will never recapture again. Chasing our past or living in the past obscures our rational thinking. In my case, I was still chasing after the love of my father through what's commonly called "rebound relationships." For those that may not know, rebound relationships are when you use another man to get over your Ex, which can have very dangerous consequences. However, my Ex-husband and I had separated he lived with his mother. My daughters and I lived in our home. Mind you back in the day, separating was a divorce. In my mind we had divorced a long time ago, I felt my actions were justified. Nonetheless, in the process of this separation and my rebellion I lost my good job with benefits at Hamilton Family Health Center as a Medical Receptionist.

I then started working at this factory where I met the next depiction of my father. What drew me to him was his kindness and attentiveness, there was no physical attraction. I didn't own a pair of sneakers because I loved to dress up, I would always wear casual shoes to work in this factory. He noticed, and he approached me to ask what size shoes I wore. I thought why this strange man asking me what size shoes I wear. I said why? He says, no disrespect I just want to know what size shoes you wear because I see you're wearing dress shoes to work. I told him I don't own a pair of sneakers. I eventually gave him my shoe size. The next day he came to work with a pair of sneakers he had purchased for me. Then we started having lunch together. He had a great sense of humor. Which was an attraction, as well. I love to be around people that make me laugh. Laughter was and still is my medicine. As time went on, we became close; he changed my entire situation. There wasn't any conversation of him becoming my man, he just became my man. My daughters loved him because he was also kind to them. He knew I was separated, but at the time that wasn't a concern of mine or his. He tried on many occasions to get me pregnant. I didn't know that he was trying until I became pregnant. He told me I've been trying to get you pregnant for a long time because you're going to always be attached to me. Women are not the only ones that play those games. Red Flag number one! Then he began to show the other side of himself when he felt he had me. Then I started hearing of him being with other women. He denied it. How I could identify that he was with someone was by my body, I was very sensitive I would get bacterial infections and other sexually transmitted diseases as well. Red Flag number two: allow me to back up a little to get to this next red flag, when I attended hair school, he was a great supporter there. However, when I finished hair school, I decided to get my own hair salon. He helped me with the internal construction of my hair salon, I then became pregnant again and had my other son. Now I have had two children by him, and I'm still married. He asked me several times when I was going to get a divorce and I told him sarcastically when I wanted to. I was still with him, but I wasn't going to marry a womanizer! I used my marriage as a safeguard and an excuse. I could go on and on but let me get to the point.

Circumstances did eventually change, and I did get a divorce after my second son, but not for him for me. I began to feel guilty. Nonetheless, I had a stylist working with me in the salon who I also went to hair school with. Someone told me that he was seeing her. I confronted her and she told me she had been with him. Let me tell you how I know she was telling me the truth, because if you know anyone that has ever had a bacterial infection it has a terrible odor, it smells like fish. One day we picked her up for school and I smelled her. I had just got over the infection myself. I never told anyone these details because it was truly an embarrassing experience, but it's the truth. I pray my transparency helps someone. Nonetheless, we were at the salon, and I couldn't wait until he pulled up. She and I went outside confronted him and he denied it right in her face. He said that didn't happen. I knew he was lying, this was adding fuel to the fire at that point. I was trying to make away for my escape. That's not all, one day her sister was in the salon getting her hair done. She didn't know who he was to me, she said who he come in here to see? I was with him last night at the strip club! Red Flag number three: and the final straw! I didn't say anything to him there, I waited until we got home. When I confronted him, of course, he lied. Consequently, this is was my first experience of physical abuse. He knew it was over, he hit me in the face and gave me a black eye. I started fighting him back. Imagine, he hit me, on top of that for something he had done! I can't explain how I felt, I had heard about women getting physical abused. However, this time it was me! I put on a wig with a swoop bang that would cover my eye. What I can remember saying, "So this is how it feels to be in a physical abusive relationship?" All kinds of emotions were stirring up in me. Fear, worthlessness, degradation. What I did know is that I wasn't going to live like that. His behavior would repeat itself if I allowed this! He was going to keep on doing it. I told him I was done, I put him out, but it wasn't that easy to get rid of him! My children had gone out of town over my sister's house, I only had one child with me, which was my baby boy. He wasn't allowed to come to the salon so one night after I had gotten off work, I went home locked the doors and the screen door because he still had a key. I was on the phone talking at that time with a so-called friend of mine in my bedroom, with my son lying beside me asleep. He cut the screen door and snuck in quietly. He hid all the landline phones. I heard him and quickly got off the phone. Consequently, he still heard me on the phone. He said, who are you talking to? I said nobody. He became furious! I jumped out of the bed because I knew it was going to result in a fight, and I was prepared to fight him back. I heard a voice say don't hit him back. That voice was God, I got in a fetal position covering my head and face as he began to hit me with all his might. It felt like baby taps. He notices me not fighting back then he stopped. I got up and ran into the closet. I don't know if you remember this toy phone called the "Speak and Say?" However, it was an actual telephone with a phone jack. I found it, plugged it up in the kitchen dialed 911. He ran out of the door. I called my so-called friend back and he came and got me, and my son. He took us to a hotel where I stayed for the remainder of the night.

Depiction Number Three:

The devil wasn't done with me yet. That friend! My Ex told me not to talk to the guy that owned the barber shop next to my salon. There was a reason why? He would get his haircut there and they knew all his business. When my Ex started getting caught it wasn't coincidental it was a set up. The guy at the barber shop would send messages through another guy I had working for me, we called him Shaky Tone. He noticed that Shaky and I were close. He used him, believe me it wasn't for free! He had to pay Shaky to do it. You see Shaky was on crack! He would have done anything for money!

On top of that, he didn't care for my Ex, Shaky gave him all the ammunition he needed. My so-called friend had an agenda as well. His reasons for exposing my Ex he said was for my benefit, he told Shaky: "You're just going to let him kill her!" However, it was for his own selfish motive. Remember earlier I told you about the guy that I assumed knew the Word of God? This is him! Due to what I was currently going through, I vowed I wasn't entertaining any more sexual activity unless I was married. He pretended to respect that, and we continued to be friends. We went out on dates and spent a lot of time together. I began to get comfortable within our friendship, which was his plan. He was very patient. I told you what attracted him to me was his knowledge of God. Let me fast forward to what led to me to almost having a nervous breakdown! This was the man I ultimately married. However, this is where the rubber met the road! The very thing that attracted me to him was the very thing he used to torture me with: The Word of God! In addition, the first time he reared his ugly side! We had gone to the grocery store; myself, my children along with him. Upon returning home, we began putting the groceries away. Someone erroneously placed the frozen French fries in the cabinet, and he became furious! Yelling, screaming and cursing at my children! I couldn't believe he went there over a simple mistake! I confronted him about cursing and yelling at my children, I said: "You might have put those fries in the cabinet yourself, it's not that serious!" Man, I guess I insulted his intelligence, he said: "B (Profanity) I didn't put those fries in the cabinet!" When he called me out of my name, it felt like he punched me! It went to the depths of my soul! I told him: "I'm not your B!"

Let me tell you, no I MUST tell you this! One day he was speaking on the phone with his mother. He was furious with his mother because of something they were discussing, and he called his mother a "B" (profanity) and I heard him. I said to him word for word: "If you called your mother a "B" and that's your mother, every other woman is a B!" He would later apologize, but that blatant disrespect was in him. Nonetheless, he had plenty more episodes of rage! I would try to justify his negative actions because of his abusive upbringing as a child. I later had a daughter by him, she was a baby. My other children told me not to marry him. I can remember my oldest son in the driveway the day we were going to the courthouse. I will never forget the look on his face and the tears rolling down his cheeks. He was only about 5 years old. Even as I'm writing this, there's still a tender place in my heart because of the aftereffects it had on him. Truthfully, all my children for that matter. I should have listened to them. However, my sole reason for marrying him wasn't because I loved him, it was because I didn't want to fornicate anymore. He was the one I was with at the time. I know I wasn't in my right mind, because when we separated, I didn't even know his age these are the effects of a rebound relationship.

My children and I started attending the church that we discussed earlier with the First Lady I met in the salon. I went to her for advice. I told her my convictions and that I could repent for everything except fornication. I was clearly under conviction, it really bothered me! We did try unsuccessfully living together without having sex, but that certainly didn't last long! Her advice was for me to marry him. I had respect for her opinion, and I married him. She was aware my former husband had a problem with her and her husband. He was trying to stop me from attending their church. He told one of his friends he was going to do everything possible to get me out of that church! He would torture me with the Bible! He would actually hem me up in the bedroom and make me listen to him. If I would try to leave, he would swing his fist real hard back and forth and tell me to walk through it! "This is the only way you're going to leave!" He would hem me up wherever I was, in the kitchen, at my job, in the car on the way to work. If I wasn't with him, he would call me on the phone constantly, back to back. He would throw the Bible at me and say you will listen to that preacher, but you can't listen to me. He would also call them by their first names as a form of disrespect! Thankfully, something was a little different this time because of my growing relationship with God. In 2003 my life began to change not only did we get married in 2003, I felt God's drawing power I was baptized before I got married and shortly after I received the precious gift of the Holy Spirit. When I was filled with the Holy Spirit, I was so excited that I told him. His response was negative. He would say: "Do it, let me hear!" He was mocking me. I told him it doesn't work like that. The most fulfilling moments in my life came from my relationship with God however, I couldn't share it with him. As you can probably tell, when I finally came back to church, I was desperate! My daughter was acting up so bad I told her I was going old school on her. She thought I was going to beat her, whipping her wasn't working, I took her to church. I've been with God ever since. I allowed my Ex-husband to be him and I started doing me! God began doing a major transformation in my life! I am eternally grateful!

Depiction of my Heavenly Father:

Praying was indeed my saving grace! Evangelist Hicks and I met at the church I was attending, she and I became good friends. One Sunday she preached a sermon on the importance of prayer. I will never forget it, The Word was timely, and it resonated in my soul. I would attend every prayer service no matter what time it was. It was through my prayer life God revealed to me those three relationships I experienced were three depictions of my father. Unfortunately, everything I remembered about my father was negative. My father was an alcoholic, he was abusive, verbally and physically to my mother, and unstable. We moved all the time. Additionally, he was possessive, a whoremonger, and would become very angry to the point of rage. All three of them were wounded from their past, as my father had been! They each had a version of him. Those spirits were familiar spirits, drawn to me because of an unfulfilled void. The start of this battle with these three men from my past transpired from the ages of 19 until I had my 40th birthday. I separated from my former husband and moved into the apartment. My 40th birthday fell on a Sunday that year. We were at church enjoying testimony service. They asked me if I had a testimony. Yes however, all I could say at 40 years of age was that I finally felt FREE and that I had begun to know my worth! I raised my hands up high above my head to signify that my expectations were at a higher standard at this point in my life! No more settling for less, no more compromising God's standard! I was NO LONGER this abandoned, thrown away child I thought I was and had previously centered my life around! I am someone's child, I am a child of God! Which spoke volumes for a person like myself, coming from 39 years of bondage and not knowing who I was! Victory!

TRANSFORMATION INTO A VIRTUOUS WOMAN:

I was in the right place for God to perform a miracle; broken-hearted!

Someone quoted:

"Those that are broken hearted have discovered that they cannot control their own lives, because they are inwardly shattered and therefore need Divine help."

God prefers us to be broken. I was tired I had reached my rock bottom. My time of "chasing Jason" was over, my REAL chase began! Chasing after God and my dignity. I was prepared to do whatever it took. Unlike Naomi, (in the Book of Ruth) I didn't blame God. God was the one who revealed the signs to me. It was through my ignorance, that I couldn't recognize them. It took those tragic and devastating relationships to truly appreciate this point in my life. I had declared on many previous occasions I was not going to be sexually active until I got married. It's easy to fall back into bad behaviors. However, this time I meant it! You've heard of the Laws of Attraction? It is the belief that positive or negative thoughts bring positive or negative experiences into a person's life. I came to understand that I was attracting men equivalent to what I thought of myself. Additionally, I didn't have the knowledge to choose. If you want to make better choices, and change your attraction to A Man Of Godly Character you must increase your value.

"Choices are determined by value or the lack thereof." -T.D. Jakes

By the help of the Lord and a made-up mind, I wasn't going to make this mistake again. So, I had to reevaluate my life, change my thought process. One thing I noticed I hadn't been by myself since I left my mother's house. Like I said earlier, I had conformed my life around the men, and my children I didn't know who I was. For me to add value to my life, I first had to understand who I was; and be willing to die to the old me to live. I had many issues that I needed God to deliver me from to become this woman of virtue, let's start with TRUST. God's ways are truly past human discovery! God is simply amazing! He knows exactly what you need, and how to get you to the place to get what you need! He does it at the appointed time! God is a set up God, He planted me in this church for a reason, beyond what I originally thought. My first example of how a man was supposed to treat a woman "A Man of Godly Character" was exemplified by my Pastor at the time, and his wife; and also, another couple that attended the church. Not only did they both have respect for their wives they had respect for all women, and their wives didn't have a problem with that, as far as I could see. I had a problem receiving hugs. my pastor he would grab me and hug me so tight; at first, I would resist him. His wife finally told him; Tricia has a problem with hugs. God used him in this ministry! His hugs were breaking something in me. Those hugs were hugs of love, with no strings attached, like hugs from a father. As far as I can remember I had never been hugged by my father! Every other man had an ulterior motive when they would embrace me. Moreover, my trust issue was so severe, and so deep, God Himself had to tell me, LET ME LOVE YOU! What the devil meant for bad, God will turn it around for your good. The very thing the enemy tried to use for my demise (men) God used to help heal me! God placed some awesome men of God in my life to show me not all men are evil or mean you harm.

Most importantly God! Let me give you another example. One day I was driving Uber it was getting late, I picked up this couple who were going out to dinner. The guy says to me: "Are we your last customers?" I said, "I may go home after you guys." In my mind I was thinking I need to make a few more dollars, but it is getting late. Nonetheless, we had a great conversation while in route. When I reached their destination, he gave me a big tip and said, "Go home it's getting late." The voice tone he used, and the way he said it, was like a concerned father speaking to his daughter. I knew it was my Heavenly Father speaking through him. God knew exactly what I needed! He is many things, but I needed Him in the position of what I had been yearning for, a father! Now my view of men, as a virtuous woman, is NOT centered on my earthly father and feelings of: abandonment, pain, resentment, worthlessness. It's centered on my Heavenly Father, and emotions of: Love, Joy, Peace and every likeness of the Great I AM! His Divine qualities and principles. A good Father and that's who He is, The Psalmist David says He's a good, good Father! He doesn't give his daughter to anybody, he has to be worthy of her favor. Can a wayward woman become a woman of virtue? Absolutely, through prayer, Luke 18:1. Through God's Word, Hebrews 4:12, as well as Him via God's Holy Spirit, John 16:13. This is what transformed me to become a Woman of Virtue. In addition, Jesus had many women followers who were at one time before they met Jesus wayward women. He will do the same for you!

I previously conducted this series on our teleconference Prayer Line called "The Woman!" It's where this book was derived from. Since God directed me to this theme and the sharing of my personal testimony, I would like to include the brief testimonies of some of the ladies that were a part of this Prayer Line Ministry and conversation and their results:

"The Woman" was a powerful series and a steppingstone for me in deliverance! It reopened some wounds and then healed them at the same time! This was unpleasant because these memories were pushed back in my brain and wrapped in a cocoon. I didn't want them to resurface; I wanted the healing, but not the exposure. The Word unlocked and exposed everything I didn't want exposed: relationships, generational curses, marriages, and sexual sin. All manner of sin and emotional battles that most women go through and never receive healing. Most of the women hurting are in the body of Christ. There were many deliverance sessions for me, and they are still coming, but "THE WOMAN" opened me to see me through God's eyes. The Woman is an ongoing series for all women, it is a lifelong lesson that increases day by day." – Sister Soldier

"Before being apart of this ministry, I was dealing with issues I had suppressed since my teenage years and carried into my adult life. Instead of dealing with the issues, I became bitter and angry towards men, hearing other women's testimonies and the biblical teaching of Pastor Taylor, it allowed me to share openly without feeling guilty or shame. Once I verbalized the things that made me angry; I asked God first, to help me to forgive myself and second to forgive the ones that hurt me. Once, I acknowledged that I wanted to be delivered from being angry, the healing process began. The one thing I love about Pastor Taylor is that she is not judgmental, she listens, she corrects, and she always gives God the glory!" -Sister Joanne

"We went through a series called "The Woman" that helped me understand so much about myself. I learned about marriage and how to be a better wife. It also showed me how to help my husband, support him and at the same time make sure that we are both getting what we need from each other. Additionally, how to deal with situations when they arise and to understand that the enemy will at times use your mate against you and to know the difference. I was also taught how to develop a personal and intimate relationship with our Lord and Savior Jesus Christ. I have experienced Jesus in ways that I did not imagine I ever would. Through the studies I've learned how to surrender to Christ and trust Him. I've learned how to wait on the Lord! This has been the best thing that has happened to me. It's a wonderful feeling to experience the perfect peace of The Lord." – Sister Janice

CHAPTER 8

DEPRESSION IS A MENTAL ILLNESS

Experiencing anguish, trauma, and abuse, along with varying levels of dysfunction for most of my life has affected my mental health. God exposed the root of my issue, as previously stated, was ABANDONMENT. Abandonment produced other attributes, rejection, codependency, low self-esteem, wrath, bitterness, lack of love, childhood depression, which transitioned into adult depression. I did not know of this until God himself revealed it to me. How God revealed it to me was through someone very dear and close to me, my mother. My mother held on to unforgiveness, as I told you earlier for over forty years. As a result, she suffered from many physical and mental ailments. When my mother passed away, I found books on depression. I was aware of her physical infirmities, but I had no clue of her mental state. Most of the people that suffer from depression don't realize they have it because they do not know the symptoms. Those that are close to those that suffer are oblivious to the signs as well.

Nonetheless, I just thought she was crazy, lazy, and mean. Unconsciously, that lady I grew up with, I was becoming! I had resentment for my mother and admired her at the same time! That's when I discovered myself becoming bitter and depressed, and I didn't want to live the duration of my life like that. My mother had an issue with men because of the unforgiveness she had for my father. As a result, this kept her in prison to him. And it altered her life. That same man, if I continued on that self-destructive path, would change my entire life as well. I refused to allow him to continue to have that same power over me as she allowed to have over her. I had already given him many years. I chose to forgive my father. And every other man that had ever done anything to me, with the help of the Lord. I had to stop playing the victim. I loved my mother, but I prayed to God not to have the same results she did.

Moreover, God showed me for me to break that generational curse. I must do something different. If I continued in the same pattern, I was going to get the same result! I watched my mother struggle with her weight. A sign of depression, as a child, I would overeat too. I would eat until I got sick to my stomach. This behavior continued until I entered adolescence. When I became a teenager, I didn't stop, but I didn't want to be fat, to be honest, I despised becoming fat. However, I wanted to eat; I began to make myself vomit.

Consequently, when I looked in the mirror, I saw myself bigger than I was, and I wore a size zero when I was in middle school. Nonetheless, I didn't like the way vomiting made me feel, so I started using laxatives to get rid of the food. The medical term for this disease is called Bulimia. At the time, I didn't realize that this eating behavior had a medical name. As an adult, I stop taking the laxatives as often as I was, and I then became obsessed with working out. I recall, as a child, I had no interest in my health/wellness, like practicing good oral hygiene, i.e., brushing my teeth, taking a bath, etc. Besides, I didn't care about my education either. I didn't like to fight, but I would always get into fights. It wasn't until my second divorce and my mother's passing that God began to take me through my deliverance process(es) and expose the root of my abnormality and its behaviors. I did a series on the Prayer Line, which I will get into more detail later in the chapter: deliverance by identifying the root. Depression is a mental illness that can result from a deep-rooted issue, suppression, an unresolved issue, hereditary, environmental, trauma and loss, etc. Before someone can genuinely be delivered, we must FIRST identify the root cause, symptoms/attributes. On the Prayer Line, I gave the symptoms of Adult Depression as well as Childhood Depression. Most of these behaviors were experienced as a child; they simply went undiagnosed and undetected.

Types of Depression:

- Major

- Chronic

- Atypical

- Post-partum

- Bipolar

- Seasonal Psychotic

Symptoms of Adult Depression:

1. Depressed mood most of the day feeling sad or empty, tearful

2. Significant loss of interest or pleasure in activities that used to be enjoyable

3. Weight loss or weight gain, decrease in appetite

4. Difficulty sleeping (insomnia) or sleeping too much

5. Agitation or slowing down of thought and reduction of physical movements

6. Fatigue or loss of energy

7. Feeling worthless or inappropriate guilt

8. Poor concentration, Having difficulty making decisions

9. Anger

10. Isolation

11. Anxiety

12. Thoughts of Death (Suicidal)

Symptoms of Child Depression:

1. Irritability or Anger

2. Continuous feeling of sadness, hopelessness

3. Social withdrawal

4. Increase sensitivity to rejection

5. Change in sleep patterns

6. Vocal outburst or crying

7. Difficulty concentrating

8. Fatigue and low energy

9. Change in appetite increase or decrease

10. Physical complaints

11. Reduced ability to function during events and activities at home, with friends, in school activities, hobbies, and interests.

12. Feeling worthless or guilty

13. Impaired thinking or concentration

14. Anxiety

15. Thoughts of Death or Suicide

Studies show symptoms of depression in children vary. It is often undiagnosed and untreated because they are passed off as normal, emotional, and psychological changes that occur during growth. Early medical studies focused on masked depression, where a child's distressed mood was evident by the child acting out in an angry behavior. The earlier the symptoms are detected, the better it can be managed. My understanding of this didn't come by way of a medical physician. It came by way of The Chief Physician, God. God led me to research mental illness to get a better understanding of myself. Before I started the Prayer Line four years ago, God told me that there was a mass amount of people in the church and the world depressed. Depression is one of the leading causes of death that remains overlooked in society, resulting in suicide. Back when I began to study depression, the statistics say suicide is the 10th leading cause of death in the U.S. In 2017, over 47 million Americans died as a direct result of suicide! There were an estimated 1.4 million reported suicide attempts. For girls and young women, suicide rates have mostly followed a steady upward trajectory since 2000, roughly doubling between then and 2017. 90% of those who died by suicide had a diagnosable mental health condition at the time of their death. In 2019, the suicide rate increased tremendously; unfortunately, what was unheard of, is now prevalent to this day and age, even elementary students are committing suicide! There are many ways to commit suicide. As for me, I wasn't putting a gun to my head, taking pills, or any of the obvious things that people do to commit suicide. My suicide attempts, as well as others, were social; social suicide. Let me explain what that is, unconscious acts that it produced through excessive behavior (sin), which produces an action. People don't die from having sex. Sex is a positive emotion. They die from the consequences of having unprotected sex or having sex out of wedlock (sexual promiscuity.) There is such a thing as "slow death." Suicide is self-inflicted by using vices and alternative methods to console your hurts, pain, and some say their nerves. Also, doing things that are harmful to your health that will cause sickness or maybe even death. For example, my depressed behavior was overeating. Over a while, overindulging or binge eating can cause health issues. I personally never resorted to alcohol and cigarettes, but let me share the health effects:

- Weight gain

- Cardiac issues
- Kidney issues
- Liver damage
- Diabetes

Alcohol (Causes Damage To :)

- Liver
- Heart
- Pancreas

Cigarettes

- Lung Disease
- Cancer
- Emphysema
- Chronic Bronchitis.

Depression is being stuck in the past of your thoughts. And anxiety is fear of the unknown - Therapist

We spoke about influence in an earlier chapter, let me reiterate a moment in the Book of Romans Chapter 6:16. Paul speaks about being a slave to something. Something is meaning sin or righteousness. Both produce as we talked about earlier, a behavior. Additionally, an action with consequences.

Romans 6:15-16 (NIV)

"What then? Shall we sin because we are not under law but under grace? By no means! Don't you know that when you offer yourselves to someone to obey him as slaves, you are slaves to the one whom you obey-- whether you are slaves to sin, which leads to death, or, to obedience, which leads to righteousness?"

To my understanding, a slave means someone's legal property, and they are under that person's control. Apostle Paul says in this scripture, we are going to be under someone's control. That is determined by who we choose to obey. I was a slave to my issues with my father, who had power over my decisions, actions, thoughts, responses, and behavior. The devil was trying to use me unconsciously to kill myself, BUT GOD!

Romans 6:17-18 (NIV)

"But thanks be to God that, though you used to be salves to sin, you wholeheartedly obeyed the form of teaching to which you were entrusted. You have been set free from sin and become slaves to righteousness."

Paul had a profound revelation about sin and righteousness, its affects, effects, and influences.

(Please continue reading :)

Romans 6:19-22 (NIV)

"I put this in human terms because you are weak in your natural selves. Just as you used to offer the parts of your body in slavery to impurity and to ever-increasing wickedness, so now offer them in slavery to righteousness leading to holiness. When you were slaves to sin, you were free from the control of righteousness. What benefit did you reap at that time from the things you are ashamed of? Those things result in death! But now that you have been set free from sin and have become slaves to God, the benefit you reap leads to holiness, and the result is eternal life."

Paul is speaking about what I mentioned earlier, "slow death suicide." The things we were doing in obedience to our sin nature were resulting in death. The devil uses us to kill ourselves; what we do in compliance with righteousness results in eternal life. I want you to think about it. We may have thought our actions were rational, emotional, and psychological behaviors that came from our thoughts.

The reality is, our efforts are derived from a source beyond our capability to think! We were doing what that (carnal) nature desires/draws us to do.

Romans 8:5-7 (NIV)

"Those who live according to the sinful nature have their minds set on what that nature desires; but those who live in accordance with the Spirit have their minds set on what the Spirit desires. The mind of a sinful man is death, but the mind controlled by the Spirit is life and peace; the sinful mind is hostile to God."

Sin has a nature as well as righteousness. They both have attributes; they both lead and produce benefits and result in some kind of outcome, be it positive or negative.

"Every action has an equal and opposite reaction" -Newton's Law of Physics

Romans 6:23 (NIV)

"For the wages of sin is death, but the gift of God is eternal life in Christ Jesus our Lord."

HOW TO MANAGE DEPRESSION

I am not a counselor. However, when I finally went to a counselor, they thought I was schizophrenic. During my intake, they asked several questions, and one of them was how I knew I had depression. I told her the truth, "The Lord told me." She recorded my answer, and then they scheduled me with the examiner. She is the one that prescribes and distributes the medication. When I went to my appointment, she asked me if I wanted medication, I told her no. I began to tell her how I was maintaining, through Prayer and God's Word and on the Prayer Line. The examiner told me she read my chart and couldn't wait to meet me because she thought I was schizophrenic. When I told the intake person, the Lord told me I had depression. She realized I wasn't schizophrenic, and she began to confess she was a Christian as well, and we began to talk about the goodness of the Lord! The lady told me she couldn't share that with everybody. After our conversation, she agreed I didn't need medication. Her recommendation was counseling. My next appointment was with my counselor, and my counselor was a believer as well. I know some people are reluctant to see a counselor, as I was. However, even though it was short term, it served a purpose. God placed me with believers; I spent the time there, talking about who I love: God and my children. Also, my current situation at that time. I was still homeless, living in my daughter's house with 13 people! There was another couple she allowed to stay with her, to help them get back on their feet. I would sleep or stay in my car to escape the chaos. God knew what I needed! God has put professionals in place outside the church, i.e., Physiologists, Counselors, and other trained specialists, to help with specific situations that many local churches are not qualified to help. We have far too many suicides in the church to believe that's the ONLY WAY! Some cases simply MUST go beyond prayer! God will lead you to exactly what you need. Also, KNOW your triggers! A trigger is an event or circumstance that will cause a person to go into a depressed state. Or relive the trauma all over again. Knowing my triggers is another way God showed me how to manage depression. For example, being in a hostile environment and being displaced (homelessness) are triggers for me! Dwelling on my past relationships can also trigger depression. I'm aware, and I can catch myself from going into a crisis. Additionally, if I notice myself overeating, that's also an indication that something is wrong. One of the ladies from our Prayer Line Ministry was seeing a therapist. Her family has a history of mental illness. Her counselor noticed a drastic improvement in her countenance and behavior. She asked her what she was doing differently. The therapist says, "I need some of that!" She told her she was on the Prayer Line daily, receiving prayer and The Word of God! Consequently, because of her results, the therapist joined the Prayer Line! What an incredible testimonial! There was a method that God gave me. He showed me the power of Confession: *James 5:16*, Corporate Prayer: *Matthew 18:19*, Testimonies: *Revelation 12:11*, and The Word: *Matthew 4:4* are ALL critical to our deliverance! Every

Thursday, we would have Testimony Service! The Bible says we overcome by the blood of the Lamb and the word of our testimony! Testimony Service is not only a blessing to the hearers, but it's also a form of deliverance for the person giving the testimony. Just as it is helpful to me and the others, I pray that it will do the same for you, the reader. I want to encourage you today. There is nothing to be ashamed of. Get the help you need, your happiness, wellness, and deliverance depend on it!

- Prayer
- God's Word
- Confession (Testimonies)
- Knowing Your Triggers
- Professional Counseling

Please consult your Healthcare Provider immediately if you're feeling suicidal or call the National Suicidal Prevention line at 1-800-273-Talk (8255).

No matter what anyone says contrary, **YOU MATTER TO GOD!**

CHAPTER 9

DELIVERANCE BEFORE SUBMISSION: FIRST THINGS FIRST

*D*eliverance is a journey in and of itself! Some issues take longer than others to recover. That's one key reason we have no right to judge one another. Why do women have a problem with submitting to God? To their husband? There are several reasons many women have this issue. One of the topics we spoke about is the Trust issue. When something traumatic happens in our lives, for example, verbal abuse, rejection, rape, molestation, parental abuse, and loss, to name a few, these offenses affect our lives and how we view the world. Especially if those issues are unresolved. Unconsciously, they linger and occupy a space in our hearts and minds until confronted. Unfortunately, as we discussed earlier, its presence dominates and influences our lives, governing the future. Subsequently, another misfortune, if our offender/perpetrator is a male. As a consequence, it could make it very difficult to submit to our husband. I would find it even harder if your offense originated from a loved one, father, brother, or husband. Those you confided in and trusted once upon a time. Most women's first experience of hurt occurred when they were a little girl, from their father. Statistics say there is an "absentee father crisis" in America today. According to the U.S. Census Bureau, 19.7 million children, more than 1 in 4, live without a father in the home. Consequently, there is a missing father factor in nearly all social ills facing America today. He or she is affected in the following way:

- Poverty

- Behavior Problems

- Mom-Child Health

- Incarceration

- Crime

- Teen Pregnancy

- Child Abuse

- Substance Abuse

- Child Obesity

- Education

Deliverance and healing must take place for a woman that has been affected by its impact to submit. She will not be able to give her all, for the walls that she has built around herself are there for her self-preservation and protection. Not to mention if she has children, she goes into "combat-mode" for them as well. Everyone will be guilty. More importantly, when someone has Trust issues, they don't trust anyone to a certain degree. As a result, there will be no permanent peace, and joy in their life, it will only be temporary, because that issue will keep rearing up its ugly head.

James 1:8 (KJV)

"A double-minded man is unstable in all his ways."

However, the one you must trust in is God for your healing. Also, you must forgive. If we choose to be stubborn, we will never experience the beauty of a healthy relationship.

We previously discussed how submission is established by God (*See Romans Chapter 13.*) It is an essential requirement in our relationship with both God and man. Isn't it funny how we can have trust issues, but we will give up one of the most precious possessions we have: our body (sex). Nonetheless, we must get to a place that we look at men differently to have a successful marriage. That means those walls have to come down. God doesn't have a problem blessing us with a good husband. The problem is, can we handle it? I know it has been taught that submission is just for the wife, but submission is twofold in a relationship.

Ephesian 5:21 (NIV)

"Submit to one another out of reverence for Christ."

I don't know why verse 21 has been overlooked, and we put a greater emphasis on verse 22 when it speaks about marriage. It clearly says submit to one another out of reverence to God because God is the head of the union. Everything we do is supposed to be done unto God (*See Colossians 3:7.*) Just as important, we all will have to give an account to God. God is love, and He requires us to love one another, which is the greatest of all commandments. However, we are all to have charity (love), but charity begins at home and spread abroad, as a woman of virtue, we must make sure we take care of our home. Our husband and children must know they are loved and safe. Unfortunately, this is another reason why there are many divorces in the church. Submitting to the church and our career neglecting our first ministry, our families that's out of order.

1 Timothy 3:5 (NIV)

("If anyone does not know how to manage his own family, how can he take care of God's church?")

Neglecting your household is not the Will of God. Our God is a God of Peace, and He is not the author of confusion. He does things decent and in order. Submission first begins with Him (God), one another, children, friendships, neighbors, and authority. One of the meanings of submission in the Greek is assuming responsibility and caring a burden. If the man doesn't submit as he should, it will make it hard for his helpmeet (wife) to function in her position. The two have equal authority but different roles. The word doesn't say that God gave male and female dominion over one another. You may take on his last name, but it doesn't mean you have to lose your identity, or you are a slave to your husband. In I Corinthians 11:11, the Bible speaks about a woman is not independent of man, nor is man independent of woman. That word independent means free from outside control; not depending on another's authority. It means self-governing. However, Adam (man) is to govern over his Family as God leads him with the help/aid of his helpmeet. He is supposed to have a relationship with God so he can lead his family in love, and she is supposed to allow (submit) him.

ALLOWS HER HUSBAND TO LEAD IN LOVE

Ephesians 5:32-33 (NIV)

"This is a profound mystery, but I am talking about Christ and the church. However, each one of you also must love his wife as he loves himself, and the wife must respect her husband."

Ladies, I want you to pay close attention to this verse. In this verse, the Apostle Paul is giving instructions to the husband. He says husband love your wife as yourself! He didn't say wife love your husband as yourself, or did he mention anything about love regarding the wife. Why is this? She is NOT the one that is supposed to initiate the love relationship. Women we have been out of order by initiating the love relationship, before allowing him to love us first. A man that FINDS a wife, he (the husband) proactively takes the LEAD! He's made up in his mind, to find the love of his life. We are to respect the man. You shouldn't marry anyone you don't respect. When you respect him, love will come. Ruth appreciated Boaz because of his (qualities) character. Once he finds you, allow him to prove himself. Boaz proved himself. Don't fall head over hills, and create in your mind a fantasy world, stay in reality! Then you won't be blinded and overlook some crucial attributes and or flaws.

Watch him very closely. Watch how he pays his bills, take care of his children, loves his parents, and respects women in general. Don't think you are special if he treats other women like female dogs; you will be the next female one on his list! Doing this will show you how responsible he is. It will also show you what is tolerable and what's a deal-breaker! Remember, this is supposed to be for the rest of your life; that's what your vows say! Your vows are a promise/covenant with God and your husband. That is another reason why you don't give a man or potential husband an ultimatum! If you have to give a man a demand, that's an indication, he is not ready, or he doesn't have plans to marry you. It's really up to you how many years you will put your life on hold waiting on him. Don't force him to make a choice; you make a choice. Don't relinquish your Power of Choice! When you have to place those types of demands on him, you're not allowing him to make his own decisions. When he makes the decision, he will be responsible. And you want him to love you because he chose too not because you forced him. Another reason is, you want him to commit to the vows he made for the good and the bad; this way, he has that conviction and responsibility on him. More importantly, when we use those tactics forcing someone, giving them ultimatums as we discussed earlier, those are not the attributes of a virtuous woman, so we already forfeited our identity. You took control, which will make it challenging to submit because you didn't allow him to lead in the love relationship. What will also help us to be submissive is when we know our marriage requirements. People perish because of the lack thereof (knowledge) that applies to marriage as well.

Ephesians 5:22-24 (NIV)

"Wives, submit to your husband as The Lord, For the husband is the head of the wife as Christ is the head of the church, his body, of which he is the Savior, Now as the church submits to Christ, so also wives should submit to their husband in everything."

Paul uses submitting to Christ as an example for the wives. He didn't say we should submit to our husband in some things he said in everything period. That's why it is imperative to know, respect, and trust who you are marrying. As Christ is the head of the church, meaning He took responsibility for the church. The husband has the same duties in the household. The next verse says He (Christ) gave himself up for her. What is your potential husband willing to give up for you?

Ephesians 5:25 (NIV)

"Husbands, love your wives, just as Christ loved the church and gave Himself up for her to make her holy, cleansing her by the washing with water through the word."

Christ valued others above Himself. He humbled himself unto death and gave His life in exchange for our sins; that we may have life eternal. Husbands should value their families above their selfish ambitions by putting the welfare of his family first. A husband or a potential husband should be the one who leads his family to Christ. If you are currently married and your husband is not saved or possesses humility. Pray for him to be like Christ. God will honor your prayers (See: Philippians 2:3.)

"Within the overall context of loving his wife, a husband's first and primary role in the home is to be the spiritual head, covering, and teacher. Through his words, lifestyle, and personal behavior, the husband should teach the word, the will, and the ways of the Lord to his wife and children." – Dr. Myles Monroe

Ephesians 5:27-28 (NIV)

"And to present her to Himself as a radiant church, without stain or wrinkle or any other blemish, but holy and blameless. In this same way, husbands ought to love their wives as their own bodies. He who loves his wife loves himself."

When we notice a man not taking care of himself, not loving himself, how can we believe he's going love us? When the law of marriage loves his wife as he loves himself? Like I said earlier, we have to take notice, if he's lives a destructive lifestyle, sleeping with all types of women doesn't take responsibility for his welfare, finances, and health. How is he going to take care of his wife and children? What will happen if you don't consider these things, you will end up with an adult man practicing childlike behavior. Some women believe they can change a man. A man will only change if he desires to change. Nine times out of ten, if you accept him the way he is, he's not going to change. Why should he change things if you didn't require him to change them from the beginning?

Consequently, if you decide to ignore his behavior, just know you've committed to who he is now. One exception to this premise is that God told you he is your husband! Then He has equipped you to help him get to the potential of who he has the capability of becoming. So, don't put yourselves in that position trying to change him, then you are being his God. Only the true and the living God can change him if he desires to change. I remember I was praying for God to change my Ex-husband. God told me to stop praying for him; that's my soul. I understand now; God didn't tell me to marry him in the first place. It wasn't my place to ask God to change him because he was himself. I needed God to change me! Why did I accept his behavior in the beginning? I was reaping the consequences of my own decision.

Ephesians 5:29-31 (NIV)

"After all, no one ever hated his own body, but he feeds and cares for it, just as Christ does the church. For we are members of His body. For this reason a man will leave his father and mother and be united to his wife, and the two will become one flesh."

When we unite with our husband, your friends, parents, relatives, and siblings are out of the equation. Nothing should come between you and your spouse. You have to be mindful about disclosing your business. Listening to everyone's opinion can create confusion in your marriage. You definitely shouldn't discuss your sex life and his private parts with anyone, those discussions should be off-limits. There is a proper way to seek counseling. I advise those that are not married to seek counseling before marriage as well. However, if you are already married and having marital problems before you do anything drastic, seek the advice of your respected clergy or a professional marriage counselor, or both.

Psalm 1:1 (NIV)

"Blessed is the man who does not walk in the counsel of the wicked..."

If we give all our problems to God instead of listening to everyone else, He can help us work through those seemingly impossible issues and bring about ultimate reconciliation.

Mark 10:9 (KJV)

"What therefore God hath joined together, let know man put asunder."

Submission Makes You Beautiful!

I Peter 3:2-4 (NIV)

"When they see the purity and reverence of your lives. Your beauty should not come from outward adornment, such as braided hair and the wearing of gold jewelry and fine clothes. Instead, it should be that inner self, the unfading beauty of a gentle and quiet spirit, which is of great worth in God's sight."

I Peter 3:5-6 (NIV)

"For this is the way the holy women of the past who put their hope in God used to make themselves beautiful. They were submissive to their own husbands, like Sarah, who obeyed Abraham and called him her master. You are her daughters if you do what is right and do not give way to fear."

Submission makes us beautiful in the eyes of God and your husband. Sarah, Ruth, and Esther are prime examples of the women of old that represented the beauty of holiness. Their attraction wasn't based on an outward appearance, beautiful clothes, gold jewelry, and braided hair. It was what they possessed on the inside that made them attractive. Your character speaks (qualities) louder above anything else. Not to mention, all their husbands were wealthy men. Most accomplished (wealthy) men that don't have lust issues like King Solomon, desire a woman that has certain qualities. Subsequently, an accomplished man values his image. I've heard on numerous occasions women putting down other women concerning a man's choice for a mate. "How did she get him? She isn't even cute! I look better than her!" That's because he's looking beyond looks, he's looking for a great representation (of himself, and more importantly God,) Peace and Communication – quoted from an accomplished man. Physical beauty can deteriorate in time. If someone loves you based on looks alone, he doesn't want a lifetime commitment. Looks are superficial. Additionally, it's not enough to sustain a marriage. Looks are going to fade away.

Proverbs 31:30 (NIV)

"Charm is deceptive, and beauty is fleeting, but a woman who fears the Lord is to be praised."

The accomplished man also spoke about a woman's tone. A woman can't be hardcore, loud like a man, and expect treatment like a lady. He says men find that intimidating, and it provokes aggressive behavior. It puts them on the defense. I was listening to a man of God, and he said, you can say the right thing, the wrong way, and get the wrong result! Our approach is crucial to the conclusion we desire. How you approach a person, and how you speak to them will determine the outcome. The scripture says if a man answers his wife harshly, it hinders his prayer (See *1 Peter 3:7*.) Or if a woman nags a man, it makes him want to separate (See *Proverbs 21:9*.) In discussions among a husband and a wife, the tone matters! Scripture declares a soft answer turns away wrath. When you learn how to control your tone and your energy, that will determine your response in the conversation. Apostle

Paul speaks about the woman's unfading beauty being gentle and with a quiet spirit, both of which governs our tone.

There is nothing wrong with women being strong. We can be strong, and a boss, and yet still be feminine at the same time. Moreover, it is okay if you're not strong all the time, God says when you are weak, He is strong! You have to know when, where, and who to apply your strength too. For example, have you ever tried to open a pickle jar, and it's too tight for you to open? The jar was so big, and your hands were too small to fit around the jar. Then there is someone available and competent that can assist you. Are you going to keep struggling with the pickle jar, or are you going to ask the one that's capable of opening it? What I'm saying are some things our hands are too small to accomplish. We should embrace it and appreciate each other strengths and weaknesses.

Additionally, we shouldn't put ourselves in the same category as a man. I don't believe in feminism; I think there are certain things a woman shouldn't and can't do just because of our makeup, vice versa. And there are certain things I don't want to do. I appreciate having someone to help me and someone that makes me know I'm loved, safe, and protected. In the same manner, God does. I like it when a man opens the door for me, respects me, and treats me like a lady. I don't want to be in a power struggle with my husband. I respect his position as I would like him to respect mine. God created us equal but different what I have noticed concerning men that under that strong exterior, they are sensitive beings.

SUBMISSION REQUIRES OBEDIENCE

I Peter 3:6 (NIV)

"Like Sarah, who obeyed Abraham and called him her master. You are her daughters if you do what is right and do not give way to fear."

Calling your husband or potential husband master (Lord) may be a hard pill to swallow. Before I knew what it meant, it would've been hard for me too. However, the word "master" was used in Old Testament scripture to reverence your husband. As it relates to man, the word master (LordLord, lower-case) means a superintendent of household or affairs. Also, calling their husband "lord" was a way of letting the husband know they respect their position. It's a different form of reverence when referring to God (Lord, upper-case) Yahweh, The Lord of Lord, and the King of Kings. Ultimately, God is the Lord of all. However, your husband is the LordLord (superintendent) of your household; all it means is God gave him the responsibility to take care of his home. For example, as we discussed earlier, Eve and the other wayward women went out of divine order by disobeying their husbands. As a result, massive consequences occurred, affecting their families and generations to follow. Nonetheless, "OBEDIENCE" remains as one of the core components in reciting the traditional marital vows today, along with: "to Love, and Honor."

"I am an example of what is possible when girls from the very beginning of their lives are loved and nurtured by people around them. I was surrounded by extraordinary women in my life who taught me about quiet strength and dignity." – Michelle Obama

CHAPTER 10

THE FOUR C'S

The Principle of the Four C's is an integral part of having a successful marriage or any positive functioning relationship for that matter. Everyone will not always agree on everything. However, we can agree to disagree respectfully. Marriage is a daily process, selfless work between two people learning how to be unselfish. By applying these four fundamental principles, it will help constitute a well-balanced marriage.

- Commitment
- Communication
- Complement
- Compromise

COMMITMENT

Can you remember all the things you committed to doing in life and didn't follow through with them to completion? There are specific attributes that are needed to keep a commitment. Committing is not just lip service; it takes dedication and hard work. Marriage is a serious commitment that many people take lightly. People want to invest without exerting any effort. A committed person is an individual who is devoted to the task or purpose at hand that they have committed themselves to do. Being devoted is also a character trait that you should look for in a potential spouse. These traits inform how you think about the world, overcome obstacles, and complete tasks. Modern-day society is living proof that you don't find many couples that live out their commitment until death. When you do, they are two people that are dedicated to keeping their vows. However, today there is a higher percentage of couples cohabitating without the benefit of marriage. The danger in that is that you don't have any accountability. No one has made an official or spiritual commitment. You can acquire houses, land, cars, and you will have the same rights as a live-in mistress, legally NONE!

Hebrews 13:4 (NIV)

"Marriage should be honored by all, and the marriage bed kept pure, for God will judge the adulterer and all the sexually immoral."

Some women go as far as to have children to make a man commit to them. I'm reminded of Jacob from the Old Testament scripture. Once he laid eyes on Rachel, he loved her and wanted to marry her. Rachel's father tried to pay him wages for working for him. Jacob refused the payments and asked him to let him work to marry his daughter Rachel instead. Laban and Jacob agreed for him to work seven years to take her hand in marriage. Jacob worked those seven years, what seemed like to him a few days because of his love for her (*See Genesis 29:19.*) He was excited to be able to lie with her. Finally, he waited in the tent that evening. Unfortunately, Laban deceived Jacob; he sent her his eldest daughter Leah instead. It was their custom to give away the eldest daughter. First, Laban failed to tell that to Jacob. Jacob was furious to wake up the next day to find that he had been deceived, and he didn't marry Rachel, he married her sister. Jacob could have given up and accepted Leah. However, his love and seven-year commitment weren't for Leah. Laban told Jacob he could work another seven years, and he would give him Rachel. He made another commitment for seven more years for Rachel in total Jacob worked 14 years to be with Rachel. He proved his love for Rachel. In a marriage, as we discussed in Chapter 9, the man has to love his wife as Christ loved the Church and gave himself up for her. Also, the question earlier, what is your potential husband willing to give up for you? Jacob gave up 14 years of his life, laboring for her father, Laban, just to marry Rachel. The Bible also says the wife is to respect her husband. Rachel couldn't have anything less than respect for him. Jacob is an excellent example of a man leading the love relationship.

The Number One attribute to fulfill a Commitment is:

- Love

1 John 4:7-8 (NIV)

"Dear friends, let us love one another, for love comes from God. Everyone who loves has been born of God and knows God. Whoever does not love does not know God, because God is love."

However, I should point out, Leah loved Jacob as well, but he didn't like her. The mistake a lot of women make, as I said previously. Believing you can make a man love you by having children. Leah thought that her children would provoke Jacob to love her. The one thing she had on Rachel was that she was able to have children. Rachel, at this time, was barren.

Genesis 29:32-35 (NIV)

"Leah became pregnant and gave birth to a son. She named him Reuben, for she said, 'It is because the Lord has seen my misery. Surely my husband will love me now.' She conceived again, and when she gave birth to a son she said, 'Because the Lord heard that I am not loved, he gave me this one too.' So, she named him Simeon. Again, she conceived, and when she gave birth to a son she said, 'Now, at last my husband will become attached to me, because

I have borne him three sons.' So, he was named Levi. She conceived again, and when she gave birth to a son she said, 'This time I will praise the Lord.' So, she named him Judah. Then she stopped having children."

Having children to initiate love or attachment to your husband is going about it the wrong way. All that will come out of it; is a house full of kids! Leah had six sons and a daughter with Jacob, and that still didn't change the way he felt about her. Truthfully, the way he married her had a lot to do with it. He was forced to marry her. He didn't have the love in his heart for Leah, so no matter what she would've done, even marriage couldn't make him commit. That's one reason why a married couple can't fulfill their commitment because it has to be a MUTUAL (commitment) agreement. Both parties must equally pledge the same one to another. However, a person cannot commit to you if they don't commit to God and themselves FIRST! Before Jacob committed to Rachel, he undertook (vow) to God and his purpose. *To get a full understanding of these events, please read (Genesis Chapters, 29-31).* I read this post on Instagram; I wanted to use it as a topic of discussion. The post said, "is it wrong to keep smashing (having sex) a woman who is deeply in love with you, but you have zero feelings for her?" Yes, but it proves a point that men can have sex and children without any form of attachments.

Genesis 28:20-21 (NIV)

"Then Jacob made a vow, saying 'If God will be with me and will watch over me on this journey I am taking and will give me food to eat and clothes to wear so that I return safely to my father's house, then The Lord will be my God.'"

God proved Himself, as well. He kept His commitment to Jacob. God will help us, whatever God says He will do it. God has no problem doing things for us, but just like any other relationship, He has some requirements, one, it has to be with reciprocity (mutual).

Genesis 31:41-42 (NIV)

"It was like this for twenty years I was in your household. I worked for you fourteen years for your two daughters and six years for your flocks, and you changed my wages ten times. If the God of my father, the God of Abraham, and the Fear of Isaac, had not been with me, you would surely have sent me away empty-handed. But God has seen my hardship and the toil of my hands, and last night he rebuked you."

Number Two

- Reciprocity (mutual)

Matthew 7:12 (NIV)

"In everything do to others what you would have them do to you, for this sums up the Law and the Prophets."

You have to pay attention to who you're committing too. Remember, I told you I didn't pay attention to my vows, meaning the words I agreed to. Also, ignoring the behavior of the person to who I was committing. I didn't realize when I committed; I was committing to his current condition, issues, and ethics. The total character of who he was at the time. More importantly, I was making this commitment to him before God. Vows are a set of promises, committing one to a prescribed role, calling, or course of action, typically to marriage. Solemnly promise to do specified things. For example:

Traditional Marriage Vows:

"I (insert person's name) take you (insert spouse's name) to be my wedded (husband or wife) to have and to hold, from this day forward, for better, for worse, for richer, for poorer, in sickness and in health, to love and to cherish till death do us part, and here I pledge you my faithfulness, under God's Holy Law."

Jacob made the vow to God under the conditions that He does those things he requested. When we make a vow, the expectation is to do everything that's requested. If we have no intention of doing these things, we shouldn't agree with them. God agreed to Jacob's request because He knew He could and had every purpose of fulfilling them. He is a God of integrity. When we don't accomplish the things we commit to, it shows a lack of integrity. Many of us, as I went into marriage lacking all the above. It's your integrity that's on the line, so don't make commitments with people you already know you can't live it out. Dr. Myles Monroe says, "A promise is a commitment to do something later, and a vow is a binding commitment to continue to do it for the duration of the vow. Some vows, or contracts, are for life; others are for limited periods. Myles Monroe." Subsequently, your relationship and the words you agreed to will be challenged. What's going to determine the commitment, when you are still there for each other during those trying times. That's the determining factor that you meant what you said. When someone completes the terms of their agreement for better for worse, richer or poorer, sickness and in health, love and cherish, until death do us part, they meant what they said.

Number Three

- Integrity

Proverbs 20:7 (KJV)

"The just man walketh in his integrity; his children are blessed after him."

We are not perfect, but we can be perfect in our trying (attempts.) Marriage is still a risk, something we just can't gauge or predict the outcome. We can't guarantee if a person will remain faithful. I had a conversation with this person years ago, who was a friend of the guy I was with at the time. He so blatantly told me he had been married for 16 years, and 15 of those years, he had another woman. I asked him how he was able to do that. He said, give them both what they wanted. I said to myself they don't want much. He said the other woman knew he had a wife and agreed to be in a relationship with him. On top of that, he told me he loved them both. I said how? He said you could love more than one woman. I said that's impossible because you're not supposed to give your time and attention to another woman other than your wife. He was trying to justify his actions. I believe he didn't love anyone but himself, desiring the best of both worlds (i.e., greedy.)

Another time, I walked in on a conversation the guys were having in the Barber Shop with my ex-husband, and the guys asked me a question. They said, what would you rather have a man that paid the bills or a man that's faithful? They said I couldn't have both. I told him why I couldn't have both. They said a man is going to do one or the other. I was outdone, because of this even being an option. In the traditional vows, it says I pledge you my faithfulness under God's Holy Law. Do you know a lot of people have no intention of fulfilling this part of their vows? I believe if you're not going to be faithful, you shouldn't get married. Some spouses have caught their partners being unfaithful and decided to forgive them and remain married. And that's a personal decision because people do make mistakes. However, for some women, that is the ultimate deal-breaker! Additionally, don't take him back if you don't forgive him, just to punish him, and punish her. On the contrary, you will be punishing yourself.

"Marital faithfulness involves more than just a sex fidelity. Being faithful to your wife also means defending her affirming her beauty, intelligence, and integrity at all times, particularly before other people. Faithfulness to your husband means sticking up for him, always building him up, and never tearing him down. Marital fidelity means that your spouse's health, happiness, security, and welfare take a higher place in your life than anything else except your own relationship with the Lord." – Dr. Myles Monroe

Number Four

- Faithful

Proverbs 20:6 (NIV)

"Many claims to have unfailing love, but a faithful man who can find?"

COMMUNICATION

Matthew 5:37 (KJV)

"But let your communication be, Yea, yea; Nay, Nay: for whatsoever is more than these cometh evil."

Honesty is the best policy. Saying what you mean and meaning what you say will eliminate confusion. We can't give the enemy any room or authority to wreak havoc in our relationships. He is looking for the opportunity to do so. That's why it's crucial to have HONEST COMMUNICATION. Communication is one of the most significant portions of keeping a relationship intact. Some people have no problem communicating, but it's how you convey that matters. Do you have honest communication? The majority of marriages and many relationships for that matter foundation are lies. There are numerous reasons why people lie in their relationship, and it doesn't make it right!

Here are a few reasons: (To)

- Keep the Peace

- Avoid Arguments

- Fear

- Rejection

- Afraid to say NO

- Avoid Confrontation

A dishonest foundation will not stand. You must create an nonjudgemental atmosphere for your partner to have honest communication. A fraudulent relationship is also two people pretending to be or say what the other person wants because of fear of losing them. When a link is built on lies throughout the relationship, one has to continue lying. One has to keep pretending, and this is a form of bondage as well as deception. God requires us to have honest communication as

His children. Lying is not of God; God says it's a native language of the father of lies, the devil. Those that do this belong to him.

John 8:44 (NIV)

"You belong to your father, the devil, and you want to carry out your father's desire. He was a murderer from the beginning, not holding to the truth, for there is no truth in him. When he lies, he speaks his native language, for he is a liar and the father of lies."

God can't bless a union formed on lies and dishonesty. It's equally as important to be in a relationship with someone you can be your authentic self. You MUST be honest and walk in your truth. In a marriage, we should respect each other's views and feelings. The two must create an nonjudgemental, respectful, considerate atmosphere for each other to have honest communication. It doesn't mean we have to agree on everything they say. We have to implement the practice of "AGREEING TO DISAGREE," that's Communication 101.

Another thing that prohibits excellent communication is what we spoke about in the last chapter; tone. A wise man said, "when trying to communicate with each other, a husband and wife should be careful to make sure their voices and faces agree with their words." I was on Instagram, and it so happened I ran across two men in a discussion, giving marital advice. The one guy said he had been married for nine years, and he and his wife never got into a heated argument, as far as raising their voices to each other. He says, not that they didn't disagree, they just used a non-combative tone. He also said when you enter into marriage; you don't own each other. He said the biggest mistake going into marriage is thinking that it's a contract of ownership. He goes on to say it's a contract of freedom with a person that's your friend, who you love, and want to be in a relationship with for a long time. Another example, (and this was me on every level). I would walk around the house with an attitude. Slamming doors, dishes, etc., so he could hear me, without me speaking in an audible voice. However, when my ex-husband asked what was wrong, I would say nothing. As a result, what made me mad was never resolved and became a more significant issue. Was that his fault or mine? What happened initially may have been his fault. However, when I didn't allow him to discuss it, I became at fault as well.

Additionally, my actions were merely immature. Our husband or potential husband shouldn't have to guess what's wrong with us. We have to COMMUNICATE with one another EFFECTIVELY to resolve our issues. Just as important, we have to allow a person the opportunity to be FORGIVEN.

"Communication is the ability to ensure that people understand not only what you mean. It's also the ability to listen to and understand others. Developing both of these aspects of communication takes a lot of time, patience, and hard work." – Dr. Myles Monroe

Attributes that Prevent Effective Communication:

- Tone

- Attitude

- Stubbornness

- Immaturity

- Anger

Using these fundamentals, coupled with The Word of God, will help us avoid communication break downs. It will also aid us in establishing open, honest communication in our relationships.

"Have the courage to say what you need in the moment. Most people aren't mind readers. Two things will happen: You'll either get what you need or realize that the source you are asking doesn't have the capability to deliver. Both are gifts." – Jada Pinkett Smith

Honest Communication:

Proverbs 12:17 (NIV)

"A truthful witness gives honest testimony, but a false witness tells lies."

Proverbs 24:26 (NIV)

"An honest answer is like a kiss on the lips."

Agree to Disagree:

Galatians 5:15 (NIV)

"If you keep on biting and devouring each other, watch out or you will destroy each other."

II Timothy 2:23 (NIV)

"Don't have anything to do with foolish stupid arguments, because you know they produce quarrels."

Keeping the Peace:

Ephesians 4:3 (NIV)

"Make every effort to keep the unity of the Spirit through the bond of peace."

Romans 14:19 (NIV)

"Let us therefore make every effort to do what leads to peace and to mutual edification."

Forgive to be Forgiven:

Ephesians 4:32 (KJV)

"And ye be kind one to another, tenderhearted, forgiving one another, even as God for Christ's sake hath forgiven you."

COMPLEMENT

No two people are alike. We may have similarities, but with individual uniqueness. Including different personalities, gifts, talents, etc. It takes all types of people to bring things into perfection. Subsequently, we live in a world of diversity. Instead of criticizing things we don't understand, we should embrace each other's differences. To build a house, it takes people functioning in their specific skill or trade to put it together adequately. We cannot do everything ourselves. We are not capable. That's how God made it. We need Him first and foremost because no one can do anything without Him. Likewise, and for the most part, we need each other. When God sent the disciples out to minister, He sent them out two by two. He didn't send anyone out alone. Also, He thought it not good for man to be alone, so He created Him a helpmeet. Someone to help not only him but also an accompaniment. In marriage, the two are to complement one another; they are supposed to work as a team. Teams are to achieve a common purpose or goal. It takes each player's dedication, effort, and an individual's skills to make it work. Unfortunately, everyone is NOT a team player. Those that do not negatively affect the team's performance and success. It also drags down the morale and productivity of the group. It's challenging to win or achieve your goals when you have a "non-team player" on your team. Marriage requires a team effort. You cannot have a successful marriage if one person is carrying the group alone. Two things will happen either they are going to become worn out and become nonproductive, or they will quit the team! You must do your part to enhance who your partner is and vice versa. Keep in mind the puzzle isn't complete until all the pieces are together. Besides, keep in mind what we are there for :

- Add, not take away,

- Build, not tear down,

- Compliment (each other) and not to bring complications.

Proverbs 14:1 (KJV)

"Every wise woman buildeth her house: but the foolish plucketh it down it down with her hands."

Especially if you have or desire a Godly accomplished man that is secure. He is looking for someone that will be a complementary addition to what he has already acquired on his own. What are you bringing to the table? Let me add; it doesn't always have to be financial support or anything to do with his business. Maybe he just would like you to (help) him. Boaz's choice wasn't based on her financial assets; it was her qualities (noble character) that complimented him. He watched her; how she took care of Naomi. He noticed she wasn't enticed or enticing men, rich or poor, young or old (See Ruth 3:10.) Accomplished men and money were not a temptation for her (Ruth.)

Proverbs 31:11 (NIV)

"Her husband has full confidence in her and lacks nothing of value."

Furthermore, the Kingdom of God does not function after the world's order or mathematical system, where half and a half equals a whole. In God's Kingdom, a whole make a whole! He desires two whole people to become one flesh. However, it doesn't always work like that. The reason why there are so many conflicts in marriage. We get married fragmented, and when two fragmented people get together, it becomes a more prominent, chaotic mess. I wouldn't advise anyone to get married without working on your self-development (healing) first. Meaning that a lot of people get married to fulfill a void(s), seeking things that another person doesn't have the capability of giving. What happens is that person becomes a burden to the team rather than an asset: a liability. Especially those that are carrying the weight of their past relationship(s.) Getting healed first will eliminate those past relationships dictating your future ones. Subsequently, we MUST get deliverance from our past issues to move forward into a positive, fruit-bearing marriage. Let go, release them, giving them over to God (let it go) and forgive.

- **Seek Self-Healing:**

"Her happiness is not my responsibility. She should be happy, and I should be happy individually. Then we come together and share our happiness. Giving someone a responsibility to make you happy when you can't do it for yourself is selfish." – Will Smith

What's quoted above can also bring complications and prevent one from performing as a team. Being unequally yoked, the Bible tells us do not to yoke yourself up with unbelievers. As I spoke earlier, this became a serious issue in my marriage. Our relationship with God is the most important relationship. When you're with an unbeliever, your relationship with God will become a conflict of interest. Consequently, some spouses will insist you make a choice, but to avoid all of that, be sure you know ahead of time his belief and convictions. You don't want anyone to jeopardize your relationship with God. You want them (your partner) to be an addition to your relationship and vice versa.

• **Know Who You are Yoked With:**

2 Corinthians 6:14-15 (NIV)

"Do not be yoke together with unbelievers. For what do righteousness and wickedness have in common? Or what fellowship can light have with darkness? What harmony is there between Christ and Belial? What does a believer have in common with an unbeliever?

COMPROMISE

Jesus is the epitome of compromising for the sake of love, in so much that He gave His life. In every relationship, there will be disagreements. Compromising takes two people that love each other more than they love their opinions and having their way. There has to be some compromising within a relationship. If not, it becomes a marriage without reciprocity (selfishness).

Amos 3:3 (NIV)

"Do two walks together unless they agreed to do so?"

As we spoke earlier, these things should be established in the beginning. In a relationship, one may have to do some things one doesn't want to do, go places one doesn't want to go, just for the sake of compromising and making a sacrifice to achieve harmony. For example, you may want to go out to dinner, and your spouse may wish to have a meal at home. Right here is where compromise comes in; one of you is going to have to make a sacrifice to satisfy the other one's desire. This time you may agree to stay at home and cook. Next time he may yield to what your desire is or vice versa. However, there has to be a common ground and agreement. Don't get me wrong compromising doesn't mean you have to lose your identity, respect, likes and dislikes, your voice, and opinion to appease some else. It merely means two mature, responsible adults reaching a mutual agreement. Disagreements in relationships will hinder your prayer life and your peace. A house divided cannot stand, but there is power and answered prayers in agreement. The devil loves to have couples divided because when there's division, he can conquer. Also, **HUMILITY** MUST have its work in each of you for things to flow smoothly. **Humility:** Sincerely, putting the needs and desires of another before your own. Its' a bitter but necessary pill to swallow as you grow and mature in relationship building, especially within your marriage.

Matthew 12:25 (NIV)

"Jesus knew their thoughts and said to them, 'Every kingdom divided against itself will be ruined, and ever city or household divided against itself will not stand.' "

Matthew 18:18 (NIV)

"I tell you the truth, whatever you bind on earth will be bound in heaven, and whatever you loose on earth will be loosed in heaven."

Just one of the more reasons you can't allow disputes to break down your marital relationship. Nevertheless, there are things you absolutely should NOT compromise.

- Belief(s)

- Integrity

- God's Word

- Doing Anything Contrary to The Will of God

To become a person that's willing to compromise or to be engaged in a relationship. The attribute of humility must be prevalent in your character. As it was so motivated and demonstrated by the Love of Jesus toward humanity. Humility, again: is being of modest demeanor or having a lesser view of one's importance.

- Humility

1 Peter 3:8-9 (NIV)

"Finally, all of you, live in harmony with one another; be sympathetic, love as brothers, be compassionate and humble. Do not repay evil with evil or insult with insult, but with blessing, because to this you were called so that you may inherit a blessing.

CHAPTER 11

GOD'S PROVISION FOR THE SOCIALLY AND ECONOMICALLY DISADVANTAGED

There are many reasons a person can fall into the category of becoming disadvantaged, especially women, when we lack the normal or usual necessities and comforts of life—speaking specifically of those who lack proper housing, educational opportunities, job security, and adequate medical care. Unfortunately, in society, there are double standards when it pertains to gender as well. It's known that some businesses prefer to hire men. Additionally, some companies are known to give a woman less pay for the same/equal position. Unfortunately, a person's race is also a factor that can work against many.

On one of my previous jobs, the CEO was discussing his potential applicants with another lady and me. When he was reviewing the applications, he would look for specific things. Also, when the person came in for an interview, he would look for those specifics. Which should be expected, right? However, he would identify a person according to their name; their name to him was a determining factor of their ethnic background. He would make a joke about the names of black applicants, for example, "Shaquisha" He would disregard that application immediately! Subsequently, he would also look at the gender because he was a womanizer, which made him partial to hiring women of a particular type. One lady came in for an interview, and he didn't hire her. Unfortunately, he didn't hire her because she lacked the qualifications for the job; he rejected her because she was heavyset, which was a biased or discriminatory decision.

We, as women, also experience this biased behavior in the Church/Religious Community. On several occasions, I've experienced men in leadership that wouldn't recognize me as a minister or pastor because they didn't believe in women preachers. On this one occasion, the pastor looked at my credentials and said to me we don't believe in women pastors. I will call you "Evangelist." I realized then that even in the church, this is a man's world and women have to fight to be recognized. I didn't debate with him or argue about a title, that didn't matter to me because I knew who I was. I let my calling speak for itself.

Unfortunately, this discrimination is not just limited to men; women are discriminatory against other women in ministry. Nonetheless, some women have put themselves in some uncompromising situations or have been put in intransigent cases to advance themselves and provide for their families, primarily single moms. For example, prostitution, stripping, gambling, scheming, selling drugs, and other illegal activities. In like manner, marrying someone for security reasons which often results in loveless relationships. I'm not judging them; I have indulged in some unlawful things in my past. We are a product of our environment and our current condition. Peter thought he loved Jesus so much that he would NEVER deny Him, but when Peter was put in a desperate situation, fearing for his life, he denied Jesus! Jesus foretold Peter of his future actions and forgave him! We don't know what we will do in a time of distress and desperation. However, whatever we've done, it may be hard for a man to forgive us, but God will forgive us. You know the saying: "Desperate times require desperate measures." Be careful, NOT to judge!

Matthew 7:1 (NIV)

"Do not judge, or you too will be judged. For in the same way you judge others, you will be judged, and with the same measure you use, it will be measured to you."

However, what our past behavior exemplifies is the attitude of one that lacks faith and a relationship with God. When we know better, there is an opportunity to do better. With that said, God doesn't want His queens defiling themselves in any way, for anything or anybody. Many of us are strong, independent women. Strong, independent women raised us as an example. Subsequently, being independent can be a stumbling block in our relationship with God. What happens is we have more confidence and faith in ourselves than in God. It prevents us from allowing God or anyone to help us. Don't get me wrong; there's nothing wrong with being independent; we just have to know when to apply it. There will come a time when those things that worked for us in the past; hustle, that scheme. Or whatever your situation was, it will fail to produce or work anymore. You may eventually just simply get tired of that lifestyle. Those are the times when God is trying to get your attention. I saw this with my own eyes, how God provides for those that are in a disadvantaged situation.

When my mother left my father, he was gone to work. She must have planned her escape because we transitioned right into another place. I didn't realize it then, but God promised to provide. My mother was a single parent, in a foreign location (city) with no relatives and three children. God allowed her to get a house built from the ground up. She purchased it! We never lacked food, or clothing, or ever had our utilities cut off. We had the same phone number for the length of time she lived in the house until she passed away. Having both physical and mental disabilities and without a husband, our God provided!

I, myself, not realizing what I was going to have to do when I left my ex-husband, we decided to conjoin our businesses together. So, when I left him, that meant leaving my business, leaving my income! Mind you I didn't have any food or furniture, I just got my apartment God blessed me with it was empty! Nonetheless, I was going to get my things out of the shop, and one of the church members so happened to be passing by and saw me. She knew my situation; she pulls up and gives me 300.00 for food and said, I would give me more later, and she was God sent. If you can remember in an earlier chapter when I told you God had me go to H&R Block, and I had over 4000.00 waiting on me there! Okay, in my transition, I lost the majority of my clients, and I asked God how I was going to pay the rent? He told me to use the money that I got from the H&R block. I did, my rent was 800.00 a month, and I had a few clients that I continued styling, which wasn't much, I kept a tally of my earnings. I can remember getting my yearly statement when I did my taxes, and my rent that year exceeded the money I earned. I couldn't believe it. I said, how can this be? Subsequently, this happened for two years with no late fees.

Another time when I was living in this same apartment complex, the church had a Women's Day Service, and the ladies decided to wear lavender. I didn't have the money to buy a dress. I mentioned the program to one of my clients in conversation. However, I didn't inform her that I didn't have the money for an outfit. A few days later, I received a phone call from her, and she told me God said for her to purchase my outfit, with specific instructions. He told her not to get me just anything, but to buy myself a nice expensive suit! He told her He wanted me to look as good as the other ladies. I couldn't believe it, she came and took me to Macy's and told me to pick out what I wanted, don't look at the price tag. She purchased the suit, the accessories, and the shoes. Humbly, I looked suitable for that service! I received many compliments!

God covered my children and me. The people at church had no idea what I was going through unless I told them! I kept a smile on my face! Nevertheless, God used her again, this time it was around Christmas, I didn't have any money to buy my children Christmas gifts. I had a dream! God showed me someone was going to give me 200.00. I got up didn't think anything else of it, I went on about my day my children and I were riding down the street, I believe I had just picked them up from school. When she called, she said I have been looking all over for you. She had been to my apartment; however, I thought something was wrong. She said I want to give you something, and then she asked me what I was getting my children for Christmas. I told her I didn't have any money for Christmas. She said I've been trying to get this 200.00 to you so that you can buy some things for your children for Christmas! She told me she found 200.00 in her dresser drawer and she didn't know from where it came. God had put me on her heart! I told her God had given me a dream that someone was going to provide me with 200.00, I just didn't know who or when. It blew me completely away, and she! Not only did she come over and give me 200.00 dollars, but she purchased other gifts for my children as well. I was so grateful to have her in my life. I pray wherever she is that God continues to bless her abundantly with life, health, and strength, and whatever her heart desires for being obedient to God. God will put you on someone's heart to bless you. He used her on many other occasions as well.

"One of the greatest truths of the Bible is that whenever God gets ready to do anything on earth, He always works through a person or a group of people whom He has called and who have willingly responded to Him." – Dr. Myles Monroe

During that pivotal time, God gave me a scripture to fortify me.

Proverbs 3:5-6 (KJV)

"Trust in the Lord with all thine heart, and lean not unto thine own understanding. In all thy ways acknowledge Him, and He shall direct thy paths."

I still had my struggles with trusting God because of my **STRONG** will! **TRUST IN THE LORD!** I needed to get that in my head! Leaning to my understanding, trying to figure out how God was going to do, it was an issue for me. When we learn to our knowledge or are trying to figure out God's methods, we are not fully trusting God! Nonetheless, when it came time for bills to be paid, I would declare this scripture and other scriptures to occupy my mind and gain strength from The Word of God.

My understanding was still an ongoing issue; years later, when I was homeless, this test came back again. It sounds more comfortable than it was for me. What I've learned during these tests, God will allow us to try to figure it out ourselves and let us keep bumping our heads until we get it! He is not going to stop you because it's how we learn our lesson. Just like a little child that touches a hot stove, once they experience the pain a couple of times, they become convinced! You don't have to keep reminding them not to feel that hot stove again! When they look at it, they remember it's hot. When we come to that realization, if we don't end up in a mental hospital first, that we need Him, He will be there to help us out.

Let me give you a couple more testimonies. I have so many on how God provided! I had a client that had a short haircut; she was scheduled for an appointment to get her hair done. Yet, my clippers wouldn't work. I said Lord; I have to do this ladies' hair in the morning. I need my clippers. I would turn them on, and the blades wouldn't move; it just made a sound. I didn't cancel her appointment; I went to bed that evening.

Nevertheless, when I woke up that morning, I heard the Lord say, "Put some oil on it!" I immediately got up and sprayed some oil sheen on the blades, and they began to work! Thank you, Jesus is what I said. God wouldn't allow me to miss that opportunity!

The last one, I promise! There was another time I had a bill that was due. God gave me a dream; I was at this house with some other people. I went outside, looked up in the sky, and I saw Jesus. I was so excited I ran back in to tell the people to come to see Jesus. I kept saying, "It's Jesus. It's Jesus!" Yet and still, I ended up outside by myself. As I was looking up in the sky, I gazed at Him and noticed He was wearing His crown. And He had a short beard, and there was an angel right beside Him. All of a sudden, the angel shot out of the sky, came right beside me, arched his back looked directly in my face and swooped back up beside Jesus, and I woke up! When I woke up, it was in my spirit to check my bank account, I did! There was money in my account; I believe it was 125.00! I was astounded! It still does something to me when I think about it!

I will never forget these miraculous events, and there is so much more! God loves us He cares about the little things and everything we care about and more. I'm just saying, a suit for a Women's Day Program, Toys for my children on Christmas, to add a dress I found at J C Penny's for 1.97 cents for another event I attended. He just wants us to trust Him. God's word speaks about Him being Jehovah Jireh, and what Jehovah Jireh interprets is: "The Lord will provide." This word was first mentioned by Abraham when He was going up to offer up Isaac as a burnt offering to the Lord. God provided a ram for him in the bush!

Genesis 22:13-14 (NIV)

"Abraham looked up and there in a thicket he saw a ram caught by its horns. He went over and took the ram and sacrificed it as a burnt offering instead of his son. So Abraham called that place 'THE LORD WILL PROVIDE.' And to this day it is said 'On the mountain of the Lord it will be provided' "

And then the angel said something profound to Abraham because you did not withhold your son, your only son, I will surely bless you (*See Genesis 22:15-19.*) What are we withholding from God? We have to surrender our all, even our thoughts. Our thoughts can be a hindrance to us, as was mine! It also determines the level of our faith. The way we know we have faith when we meet with a time of crisis!

Moreover, God is examining our hearts! Not by what we say: "TRUST IN THE LORD WITH ALL THY HEART." I didn't just need to get it in my head as I said earlier, I needed it (Him) in my heart! We spoke about purpose, God's plan, and living according to His principle, being a citizen of His Kingdom and the great benefits it provides. God has made a solemn promise to take care of His children. I believe God set these precious promises in place so we wouldn't be in bondage to man and the world system. Even when we thought we were taking care of ourselves in the past, it was God that afforded us the opportunity. God promises they are for the socially and economically disadvantaged. For example, fatherless, strangers, and widows. Fortunately, you will find throughout His Word the declarations He has put in place for those that fit in these categories.

The Fatherless:

In the Greek translation (Reference: No: 3737 in the Strong's Concordance), the word is "orphanos," meaning bereft of a parent or a father. In Hebrew, it means to be lonely, a bereaved person, the name is "yathown."

Windows:

A woman whose husband has died. A woman whose husband leaves her alone, frequently for a long time, to engage in usually a specified activity. The Greek word "chera," meaning a deficiency, a widow lacks a husband. The Hebrew translation refers to "almanah" which means widow and also to be desolate.

Strangers:

A person whom one does not know or known in a particular place or community. The Greek word is: "xenos." An alien, novel guest. In Hebrew: "geyr" meaning a foreigner or guest.

Scriptural Reference:

Psalm 10:18 (NIV)

He defends the cause of the fatherless and the widows and loves the foreigners residing among you, giving them food and clothing.

Additional References:

Deuteronomy 24:17, Exodus 22:21-24, Deuteronomy 10:18, Deuteronomy

27:19, Psalm 10:14, Psalm 68:4-6, Psalm 146:9, James 1:27, Proverbs 15:25, Isaiah 1:17.

GOD'S PROMISE TO PROVIDE

2 Corinthians 1:20 (KJV)

"For all the promises of God in Him are yea, and in Him Amen, unto the glory of God by us."

Fulfilled Promises:

Throughout God's Word, every promise He made, He also filled. The Lord allowed Solomon to ask Him for whatever he wanted. Solomon asked God for Wisdom to lead His people. God fulfilled His promise. (S*ee 1 King 5:12.*) He made a promise to Joshua to take the children of Israel to the Promise Land (S*ee Joshua 1:3 and Joshua 20:79)*

Joshua 21:45 (NIV)

"Not one of all, the Lord's good promises to the house of Israel failed; everyone was fulfilled."

He promised King David that He would establish the throne of His Kingdom forever (See 1 Kings 8:25.) The promises He made to Abraham God *fulfilled* (*See Genesis 12:1-3, 21:5, Romans 4:21, Galatians 3:14.*) Jacob's Promise (S*ee Genesis 5:23, Genesis 28:15-15, 30:1-25, 33:15)*

If there is anyone, we can believe that will fulfill their promises, without exception or controversy, it's God. I will give you six reasons why, with scriptural references:

- He's not a man that He should Lie

- He Does Not Lie

- He can't Lie

- He is Faithful

- His word Doesn't Return to Him Void

- He Honors His Word and His Name Above All

(Numbers 23:19, 2 Peter 3:9, Titus 1:2, and Hebrews 6:17:18, Hebrews 10:23, Isaiah 55:11, Psalm 138:2)

It should be undoubtedly clear by compelling the evidence presented that God has an excellent record! If God has spoken to you, whether in a dream, vision, through a prophet, His Word. Or by hearing of His audible voice, it shall come to pass! Time has no measure; that has no bearing here. It doesn't matter how long you have been waiting. He will fulfill His promise! It's His Name and His Word that's on the line. His integrity is impeccable!

2 Timothy 3:16-17 (NIV)

"All scripture is God-breathed and is useful for teaching, rebuking, correcting, and training in righteousness, so that the man of God may be thoroughly equipped for every good work."

CHAPTER 12

DELIVERANCE FROM BONDAGE BY
IDENTIFYING THE ROOT: THERE IS
ALWAYS A ROOT CAUSE

For us to have healthy relationships, we must confront and resolve our issues. There is always a root to any frequent, destructive, violent, and excessive behavior. Subsequently, the process of true deliverance comes by exposing the source of the problem. For example, when someone goes through a twelve-step rehabilitation program, the very first step is to speak one's name. The next step is to confess the problem. What it proposes or demonstrates is a person taking ownership (acknowledging) of their behavior, along with identifying the problem. For example, my name is blank (taking ownership) I am an alcoholic (the problem). Or whatever the issue may be, i.e., sexual addiction, food addiction, drugs, or anger, etc. However, those conditions I just identified are not the root; they are coping mechanisms. They are conscious or unconscious "cover-ups" that enhance camouflage or control behavior (defense mechanisms), which stem from the root. What is the root? The base cause, source, or origin of something. For example, if anger is your problem, what made you angry? That's the cause. Generally, it's something offensive, traumatic, or devastating that has happened in one's life. For example, rape, molestation, physical abuse. Or loss, verbal abuse, growing up in a hostile environment, etc. Confronting your issue is a gateway to exposing those issues suppressed. It's imperative in our deliverance that we come out of our secret closet and confront our hurts, pains, and our past.

The more technical term is subconsciousness. We spoke about suppression briefly in an earlier chapter. I became a professional at suppressing my feelings, which resulted in anger, depression, and food addiction. Suppression means to put an end to forcibly. To not allow one's self to feel. Our minds are so powerful we can make ourselves believe anything. However, unconsciously, those memories are not gone, and unfortunately, ignoring the issue doesn't make it go away. That is not how our minds work. Our conscious mind may comprehend to wipe away an event. However, it still exists in our subconscious mind. Our subconscious mind is what influences our behavior. Besides, some people consciously forget their traumatic experiences. They have to have therapy to remember what happened because it was such a travesty. Those events can be rehashed or resurfaced through a progressive process from their subconscious.

Subconscious: Of or concerning the part of the mind of which one is not fully aware, BUT WHICH INFLUENCES ONE'S ACTIONS AND FEELINGS.

What is a subconscious mind? Your conscious mind commands, and your subconscious mind obeys. Your subconscious mind is an unquestioning servant. It works day and night to make your BEHAVIOR fit a pattern consistent with your emotionalized thoughts, hopes, and desires. Does your subconscious know everything? The subconscious mind is a databank for everything, which is not in your conscious mind. It stores your beliefs, YOUR PREVIOUS EXPERIENCE, YOUR MEMORIES, your skills. Does your subconscious mind remember everything? Yes, your subconscious mind will not forget anything.

They are explaining why those well-kept secrets have a tumultuous effect on life. Unconsciously, our mind, body, and soul are going to respond. The same way it responds to stress and disease. For instance,

I don't want to face it. I'm ashamed. I want to wipe it completely out of my memory. I don't want people to judge me. Was it my fault? I'm afraid of what people may think about me, examples of the things that go through one's mind to keep them trapped in the rooted issue. They result in the use of coping mechanisms to try to check out of their reality and self-medicate themselves—the total of why people become addicted or codependent. As a result, if we continue to live there, we will attract other wounded people, which can become wounded projects, (servant to the injured) another form of self-medicating. One can be addicted to other people's issues to decrease the validity of their own. People becoming codependent one of another that suffers from root issues become enablers. If healed, you can help someone else. What I mean is, you will find comfort in their pain or their imperfections to make you feel better or superior; or otherwise remain in complete denial, avoiding your issues. Subsequently, there is a danger in it; that form of self-medication can also become toxic for you as well as them. Some bad relationships we stay in are because we feel sorry for them or vice versa.

Consequently, we try to rationalize who is the toxic one in the relationship, which it's both parties. Why were the two individuals drawn to one another in the first place? Familiar spirits, a commonality. Just like lust, lust attracts lust. Toxic attracts toxic. It's imperative if you desire a healthy relationship to get healed, mind, body, and soul. To eliminate one going into a relationship putting unrealistic expectations on someone that can't fulfill them. Let me say this; even an accomplished man can have issues. So, don't base your evaluation of him on his accomplishments (money). Crazy people have money and own fortune five hundred companies. People can function competently in certain areas and debilitate in others. That's why I felt it necessary to share with you Chapter 11: "God's Promise to Provide" to eliminate finances being a quest for marriage.

How to come out of the closet?

• By letting those things that we have suppressed come to the surface.

- Facing our Fears
- Coming out of Denial
- Confessing what Happened
- Confessing or confronting the person or persons **responsible for hurting us.**

We spoke about the principle of confession according to the book of James 5:16, where it says to confess your faults so you can heal. I want to reiterate this, ask God to lead you to someone to discuss your issues. It may be a therapist or someone you have no emotional ties—a professional with qualifications that are certified to deal with your particular problem. For example, if you experienced sexual assault, they have therapists that specialize in sexual assault cases. For me, I needed someone that specialized in depression and trauma. I found out through therapy why I get startled easily. That is one of the effects of someone that has been traumatized or has PTSD (Post Traumatic Stress Disorder.) More importantly, I strongly advise you to try Jesus! He has the solution needed to complete your deliverance! He doesn't do anything for temporary satisfaction, like using coping mechanisms as we named earlier. His remedy is permanent, total, and complete! His root purpose for coming into the world was to set us free from sin and our infirmities. There is nothing wrong with incorporating everything you need for your healing process. Jesus and therapy; if need be! Deliverance means to be rescued, set free, and released from bondage and imprisonment, which brings us to the next step: FORGIVENESS.

DELIVERANCE FROM THE BONDAGE OF UN-FORGIVENESS

You can't experience true liberation with unforgiveness in your heart. Unforgiveness is the principal reason issues continue to live in our subconscious mind and provoke negative behaviors, mainly because there's an unresolved issue. Forgiveness is an essential part of your healing process. Forgiveness breaks those barriers and practices (patterns) that were caused by the root. I know you've heard the importance of forgiveness preached time after time. You've even read it for yourselves. You've listened to forgiveness is not for the other person; it's for you. Also, if you don't forgive, it will cause a break down in your relationships. Unforgiveness will keep you imprisoned to the person that initially hurt you. They will continue to have power over you, and repeat that offense over and over again. Also, unforgiveness will make a person physically sick. More importantly, it prevents someone from being forgiven of their trespasses. Just as important, it will affect one's eternal life. None of these results are favorable. However, being aware of all these devastating consequences, the question remains: Why are we still dealing with un-forgiveness? Someone may not like what I'm about to say because it will eliminate all excuses. It's because we CHOOSE NOT to forgive. Also, we chose to handle it in our way. Forgiveness is a CHOICE! When you are made aware of other options, it's still your choice of what opportunity you will take. God gave my mother the option to forgive my father before she passed away. She chose to forgive him. It didn't matter how long it took her at that point because my mother had suffered the consequences of holding on to unforgiveness too long. Thankfully, she didn't allow it to prohibit her from eternal life. It's in a different category when you know something, then we have made a conscious decision to choose not to release the offense *(hurt, pain, bitterness, resentment, and vengeance)*. Some have become accustomed to the lifestyle; it has become "their normal." To forgive is to stop feeling angry or resentful toward someone for an offense. Some people have flat out said they are not going to forgive regardless of the consequences. Besides, some people have found comfort and attention in that state, and they don't want to give it up. That's truly unfortunate that some people use their hurt for care. A "woe is me attitude," which gets old and tiresome. To add, it can result in relationship losses. Nonetheless, if you are still having feelings of emotion about your past. If you still feel hurt when you hear their name or when you discuss it? That is a strong indication that there is unforgiveness there. Forgiveness comes from the heart, and if you genuinely have forgiven, it won't have the same effect on your emotions.

THE HIGHEST LEVEL OF FORGIVENESS IS TO FORGET

How does Jesus Christ forgive us? He throws our offenses into the sea of forgetfulness and remembers them no more. The level of forgiveness God would like for us to have. 1 Corinthians 13:5 says love keeps no record of wrong. When we repent, God doesn't condemn us with our past sins. If you are feeling condemned, it could only be two things. One: guilt from not forgiving yourself. You must forgive yourself; it is just as important as forgiving others. Two: the devil is trying to keep you bound to something God has already forgiven. The devil doesn't want you free, so that's a constant battle. He is fighting just as hard to keep us bound. Who the Son sets free, is free indeed!

Romans 8:1 (KJV)

"There is therefore now no condemnation to them which are in Christ Jesus, who walk not after the flesh, but after the Spirit.

Nonetheless, to achieve this level of forgiveness, one would have to possess these Three Attributes:

1. Love: God's Love

1 Corinthians 13:5, Colossians 7:22, John 3:16, Romans 5:8

2. Mercy: Compassion or forgiveness shown toward someone whom it is within one's power to punish or harm. Luke 6:36, Matthew 5:7, Proverbs 21:21, Romans 12:8

3. Grace: Free unmerited favor of God as manifested through the salvation of a sinner's bestowal of blessings. Ephesians 4:7, Hebrew 4:16, Hebrew 13:9, Hebrew 13:9, Romans 6:14

It is not an easy process, I understand, especially how the world is today. There are a plethora of reasons one could offer trying to justify not forgiving. We can have justifiable anger for injustice and forgive, not hate. The truth is there is no justification for unforgiveness! We must forgive because it's God's Law. Forgiveness is MANDATORY! Forgiveness is the premise and foundation for the plan of salvation for all of humanity. I also understand the things that happened in your life didn't happen overnight, and deliverance is a process, a progressive, continuing work in all of our lives. But, we must surrender to the process. Jesus is our ultimate example of forgiveness He is the best candidate and model! His life, earthly ministry, death, burial, and resurrection to teach us how to overcome obstacles.

My second ex was verbally abusive when we were separated; God told me to call him and apologize. I didn't understand the relevance of this because my feeling was, why am I apologizing when he offended me? My ex called that night, which presented the opportunity. He immediately began to curse me out and call me all types of names. I didn't say anything. I was crying and taking in every word. Knowing after all this verbal abuse, I'm enduring; I still have to apologize to him. So, when I could get a word in edgewise, I said whatever I have done to you in this relationship, I apologize for the hurt and pain I've caused. I apologize. He continued ranting and raging; I got off the phone. I went upstairs and got into my bed. I can't remember if I fell asleep or I was just lying there. Anyhow, God told me, now you can divorce him. I called him to let him know that I was filing for a divorce. The first thing that came out of his mouth is you owe me an apology. I told him I apologized to you last night. He calmed down and said, "are you sure you want to do this?" I said, yes! He was going to try to use that against me.

God had me express my apology so I could be free! He was perplexed; however, it was left up to him to forgive or not. Moreover, as for you, with the help of God and your dedication to your self-help plan, it can be accomplished! God's very passionate about this topic. This decision shut down my entire program and sent me to my mother's house to live for this reason (FORGIVENESS). She had allowed it to affect her life on earth, but God wouldn't allow it to determine her eternal life.

That's love! He loves you as well; that's why He gives us a chance(s) to get it right.

You hear me expounding on prayer throughout this book because prayer is my lifeline. Prayer changed the condition of my life, my heart, my thought, and attitude. God does respond to our sincere faith-driven prayers. In the Book of Mark Chapter 11 verse 22-25, God outlines the process for answered prayer. Before I give it to you, my prayer is that every woman that reads this book receives healing from all your hurts and those that caused you also hurt, that you walk in the full authority of your identity, purpose, and value—not settling for anything less than your worth. Living purposeful lives in the Kingdom of God. I pray as Oprah Winfrey once said, "that you live the dream that God dreamed for you!" Also, that God restores everything that the enemy has stolen. That God gives you healthy relationships, and beauty for ashes. God fills you with His precious Holy Spirit with evidence. That you receive the table, He has prepared for you, right in the presence of your enemies. That from here on out, you will experience joy, peace, love, and happiness now and forever. In Jesus's name! Now, take a deep breath in the Holy Spirit, take this leap of faith, and surrender it all over to God! Amen!

Mark 11:22-25 (NIV)

"Have faith in God," Jesus answered. I tell you the truth, if anyone says to this mountain, 'Go, throw yourself into the sea,' and does not doubt in his heart but believes that what he says will happen, it will be done for him. Therefore I tell you, whatever you ask for in prayer, believe that you have received it, and it will be yours. And when you stand praying, if you hold anything against anyone, forgive him, so that your father in heaven may forgive your sins."

CHAPTER 13

HOW TO BE A HELPMEET TO A MILLION DOLLAR MAN

*P*roverbs 31:11-12 9 (NIV)

"Her husband has full confidence in her and lacks nothing of value; she brings him good, not harm, all the days of her life."

Some people obtain financial status and believe they have arrived! The world would have us think we are nonexistent (a nobody) because we do not reach their definition of the status quo. The reality is that everyone matters and has relevance in God's Kingdom. God doesn't want us to focus on the things of this world because he has already established our abundant life in advance. He doesn't want us to allow stuff and things to define or consume us. We must never lose the essence of who we are as children of God. Our most precious gift from God is life John 10:10. And we should cherish every minute of it. If you have the opportunity to share your life with a significant other, that is a bonus. With that said, a man's finances have little bearing on him being a good man. A man's most valuable possession is his character. With the increase of wickedness and corruption globally, Good Godly men and women are hard to find.

Most people have an ulterior motive, the sole reason why we must wait on God. the Bible describes them as wolves in sheep clothing. If you're are blessed to have a Godly Man, make sure you appreciate him. A Man of Godly Character comes from God. He is a rare species. Far from perfect; in fact, he's an imperfect person but committed to God (first), as was Jacob. God leads him; he is sensitive to his family's needs and has the attributes of God. For you to recognize him, you must know God and His character. As we read in the previous chapter Boaz is a prime example of a Man of Godly Character (a million dollar man). A man that God chose for Ruth, he was sensitive to her needs. Also protected her virtue. This chapter is to encourage the helpmeet to build healthy relationships and implement life management skills. Characterized by the values of the Virtuous Woman. Dr. Myles Monroe says, "A solid character will reflect itself in consistent behavior, while poor character will seek to hide behind deceptive words and action."

Please don't get it confused that I'm saying that you don't deserve to be appreciated. You deserve the uttermost respect. God sees us as precious jewels, His unique creation specially formed by Him (God). Women have a history of lowering their standards, accepting abuse, and settling for toxic relationships just for the sake of having a man. That is not what God desires for His godly women. God didn't create women to be under the feet or fist of a man. He created you to be alongside Him, as we said earlier as a team. The two shall become one, joined together. Those that are married, let me ask you a question when you married your husband, were you behind him? Were you in front of him? Were you lying on the floor with his foot on your neck? No! You were beside him. So why, when you marry him, would you lower your standards and take another position. We are above and not beneath, and you help him be successful if you are functioning in your proper place. Don't get it twisted. You deserve the royal treatment. Subsequently, it is not predicated on what they believe you deserve. It is about what you feel you deserve. Most important deserves you!

Proverbs 31 is an authoritative synopsis of a God-fearing successful

Woman (wife, mother) with practical management skills, which is our guide. Helping us become or maintain a radiant, vibrant creation as we blossom on our path to deliverance, giving us the tools to prevent settling or attracting men that don't appreciate our worth, know who we are, and whose we are. The development process of strategically transitioning us above the value of a ruby God purposed us to be, is a spiritual work of art! We will be successful in our personal life, family, and business in the Kingdom of God. Establishing abundant success mentally, physically, financially, emphasizing "abundant, or in great quantity." Management is an essential piece to life's success factor, as it relates to family, business as well as marriage.

See what lousy management in the government has done to our country. Management is a skill that people spend thousands of dollars and go in debt to obtain by attending college, a university, or trade school. The college curriculum model for studying Business Management includes classes in Accounting, Human Resources, Labor Relations, Marketing, Finances, and Management, along with other specialized courses. Management is a skill and a responsibility comprised of different components to control things and people to function efficiently. It should be added to the educational program of EVERY course of study, including life and ministry! Subsequently, one can have great ideas and all the education in the world, but without proper management, it can lead to one's ultimate failure.

Nonetheless, there are specific principle skills we need to be efficient in managing our households. In similarity and on a grander scale to business management in a university, the Bible is our textbook for business management leading to productive living! It teaches responsibilities, organization, and efficiency, giving us a sound foundational structure see 2 Timothy 3:16-17. Honestly, that is where texts books derived from God's Kingdom Principles. Man, just does not give Him credit for it. One of the meanings of business: is work that needs doing or matters that have to be attended. If we neglect our business and household business, they both will be in decline like this country's government. Throughout this book, have been shared Kingdom Principles and the importance of living by God's Kingdom principles and their results. Pray to reflect on them and begin to add them to life, in this chapter, adding a few more to the list.

Nonetheless, every man has the potential to be a Noble Man. It is equivalent to what qualifies a Woman to be above the value of a Ruby, noble character. The reality is that everyone will not be a millionaire, but can still have a sustainable, successful marriage relationship. As was said, his status may not have any economic relevance, but if he has money and a noble character, he has the total package. However, some couples are not trying to be millionaires; they just want to be comfortable and happy.

Consequently, the more money made, the higher the responsibility one carries. In some cases, because the burden was so significant, it primarily caused a break down in some marriages. Factually, rich people do not have the same financial problems or fears as poor people, but they do have issues. Poor (lacking sufficient money to live at a standard considered comfortable or normal in a society) people's financial fear is how they are going to make it through to their next paycheck. Rich (having a great deal of money or assets; wealthy) people's financial fear is how they are going to keep what they have. Whichever category we are in, we need to be efficient in management.

"If we hope to become effective and successful in life, ministry, and especially marriage, we have to learn to be good managers. Stewardship means being accountable to God for every resource under our care. Effective managers do more than simply keep things running; they add value to everything they have responsibility for. Under a good manager, resources will appreciate in value."

– Dr. Myles Monroe

TAKING CARE OF OUR RESPONSIBILITIES

We should, by now, have the understanding that a marriage union is formed by the same structure as the Body of Christ. With the same expectations and principles (*See Ephesians Chapter 5*), That is why I believe it is safe for me to use Matthew Chapter 25:14-30 as an example. This passage came to mind while writing this section. It has relevance for two reasons; one, God has given each one of us responsibilities. Two, He entrusts us to take care of our responsibilities. In this parable, it magnifies the importance of taking care of our duties and its consequences when we don't take care of what God has given us. In this chapter, the Master gave out talents, (weight of silver or gold) he gave each man according to his ability. This scripture lets us know that God is not going to provide us with a responsibility we are not capable of performing. Dr. Myles Monroe says, "God never demands anything that He doesn't provide for. Whatever God commands us to do, He equips us to do." Nonetheless, He gave one man five talents, another two talents, and the other, one talent. He gave them specific instructions on what to do with the skills. The goal was to add value to what He had given them. Subsequently, out of the three, only two of them were productive. Therefore, the Master was pleased with how they managed to add value to their responsibility. The Master responded well done good and faithful servant and blessed them with more. However, the one He in which he gave the one talent, decided to bury his in the ground and be unproductive. The one token person worried about the affairs of the Master, which should not have been his primary focus. Therefore, when the Master returned, He had nothing. Consequently, the Master became furious because he didn't follow His instructions. The Master replied, "you wicked and LAZY servant. As a result, the talent he had the Master gave to someone else, and he was thrown out into darkness because he was worthless (he added no value) to the Master. All this transpired because of poor judgment and management. We hear people declare, "what God has for me is for me." However, that is true if we meet His conditions. There is substantial evidence we can miss out on opportunities, and have things in our possession, and it can get taken away. If we are not good stewards, mentally mature, well-disciplined, and prepared for it. In other words, as it relates to marriage, the Master (God) is the head of everything. He has given us our husband (household responsibilities) God expects us to fulfill our obligations to our husband (household responsibilities). If we do not meet our requirements, we become worthless (of no value) to our husband. Moreover, as it relates to confidence, he should have full confidence. However, confidence or trust is something that must be earned and developed. How we gain confidence with our spouse and God: CONSISTENCY. As Dr. Myles Munroe said, a solid character will reflect itself with consistent behavior. Due to lack thereof, in some cases, a spouse will seek to fulfill areas lacking outside the marriage. We cannot allow any room for the devil. Our significance in a relationship is the value we bring. Previously said, what are we bringing to the table/relationship as a helpmeet? Do you come to build (edify) or tear down (sabotage)? (personal assessment) Either we are going to be a burden or a blessing, we have to decide. There is a significant difference when a woman is married to a man that has acquired riches before he is married, as opposed to marrying a man that has little wealth; from a man who gained wealth with his spouse. However, what they all three have in common being accomplished men, they all desire productivity. Being lazy can prohibit productivity; the lack thereof will promote the lack of confidence in a relationship as well. One nonproductive person in a relationship can ruin what a person has established or accomplished, and future accomplishments. Would you trust your life with a lazy person? Additionally, nonproductive people will lead themselves and their partner to poverty. To add, slothfulness is a spirit (attribute) of Satan.

Slothfulness leads to poverty

Proverbs 24:30-34 (NIV)

"I went past the field of the sluggard, past the vineyard of the man who lacks judgement; thorns had come up everywhere, the ground was covered with weeds, and the stone wall was in ruins. I applied my heart to what I observed and learned a lesson from what I saw: A little sleep, a little slumber, a little folding of the hands to rest

and poverty will come on you like a bandit and scarcity like an armed man."

(*Reference Scriptures: Proverbs 20:13, Proverbs 10:4-5, Proverbs 13:4*)

Results of being Slothful:

• Lack

• Unhealthy Relationships

• Unproductive

• Financial Poverty

• Spiritual Poverty

• Poor Physical and Mental Health

• Co-dependency

• Idle

• Worthless

Efficiency is impossible if a woman is lazy with her finances, children, husband, and day to day responsibilities. A virtuous woman is not lazy. For example, where did Boaz find Ruth? He found her in the field working. Boaz saw that quality, among others in Ruth, because of her dedication to taking care of Naomi. He noticed how she took care of her responsibility. Which gave him full confidence that she would do the same for him. Also, single women with children, the burden of your children is yours. If someone said that a man would not marry a woman with kids, not right. However, he may not marry you if you do not take care of your children. I am talking about a man of good character and an accomplished man. Mind you, Boaz was rich in nobility and finances; he had the total package. However, he paid attention to how Ruth consistently treated her loved-one. Hear this, a man that's watching you is looking for specific values if you have children. Children change the narrative; there is a different expectation for a virtuous woman with children opposed to one without. A man takes a great interest in how you are treating your children that you claim to love. Our children represent who we are as mothers. If you declare to love your children and you abuse them and misrepresent them, how are you going to serve him?

Additionally, he may be looking at you as a prospective mother for his children. If you do not take care of yours, you are not going to take care of his children. Now a man with a boy's mentality does not care. A virtuous woman is industrious; she provides for her family socially, spiritually, financially, and emotionally. She is the total opposite of lazy; she is DILIGENT.

Proverbs 31:14-15 (NIV)

"She is like the merchant's ships, bringing her food from afar. She gets up while it is still dark; she provides food for her family..."

Proverbs 12:24 (NIV)

"Diligent hands will rule, but laziness ends in slave labor."

(Reference Scriptures: Proverbs 22:6, Hebrew 6:11, Proverbs 12:11)

Results of being Diligent:

- Dominion

- Wealth

- Seized Opportunities

- Profit

- Growth and Promotion

- Healthy Relationships

- Efficiency and Productivity

HOW DO YOU MANAGE YOUR FINANCES?

How you manage your finances and how you manage your finances in the time of a crisis is extremely important to maintaining. If a man is wealthy financially, one of the reasons, because he possesses excellent management skills, or he hires someone to do it for him. Additionally, even though they are financially wealthy, there may come a time of crisis. Also, this pertains to those that are not financially wealthy, can you manage your spending. Will you only spend on those things that are necessary? Remember, I told you my mother never experienced a termination of utilities, eviction, or any of those things that threaten your livelihood. She was not a millionaire, but she possessed the five-character principles pivotal to maintaining her livelihood. Also, she did not live above her means. Additionally, she knew how to itemize her spending during a crisis. We must be able to manage ourselves before we can help anyone else.

Five Character Principles

- God (provider)

- Good Steward (a person who manages another's property or financial affairs)

- Prioritization (determine the order for dealing with a series of items or tasks according to their relative importance)

- Discipline (a controlled behavior)

- Contentment (a state of happiness and satisfaction)

GOD is the source where all blessings flow. He is the provider, whether we recognize it or not. He (God) pays attention to what we do with those things He has provided (entrusted). As we said in the parable earlier about the talents, the Master is watching. There is a difference between when God delivers a husband to you, then you go and find one. With God, we must have specific qualifications. He blesses us according to our ability. If you cannot be a help meet to a man of Godly character or any man for that matter, nine times out of ten, God is not going to bless you with one until you're ready, because this type of man comes from God. If you cannot be a GOOD STEWARD over your life and finances, how are you going to be a GOOD STEWARD with someone else's? Some have gone into relationships ill-prepared end up in failed relationships. We must be marriage material. We must go through our time of preparation. Our time is the time God prepared for us individually. We are not on our friend's time, our mother's time, and society's time. We are on God's time. He knows if you are ready or not. He is (God) not going to give us things we can't handle, or we are not prepared. He does not set His children up for failure male or female. He prepares us for success by using hands-on practical training. If you are not ready, your blessing will be delayed. Everything we have experienced in our lives was and is preparing us for purpose. The scripture says if He (God) can trust you with a small thing, He can make you ruler over many. It is imperative to know your position in God. He is the first one that must approve.

Luke 16:10 (NIV)

"Whoever can be trusted with very little can also be trusted with much, and whoever is dishonest with very little will also be dishonest with much."

WOMEN OF VIRTUE

Some people's definition of a virtuous woman is based on outside appearances only; denomination, church affiliation, or attendance. I have found that to be untrue. A Virtuous Woman is not a religion its a character. It is qualities, values, and, more importantly, a relationship with God is what determines a woman of virtue. For example, Keyshia Ka'oir, I do not know what church she belongs to, or if she is even a member of a church. However, in her own right, she is a successful businesswoman and by character, a virtuous woman and example. I really can't speak for the nobility of her husband's character like she can. However, as you read a portion of her story, you will see how she helped her husband reach his potential which is the point I'm trying to convey.

Her husband has full confidence in her lacking nothing of value: She is married to a successful rap artist that goes by the name Gucci Mane. In an interview on the breakfast club, Keyshia Ka'oir discusses a challenging time in her life staying with Gucci Mane before marriage, through his prison term. During his incarceration, he gave her two-million dollars to keep for him. She talks about how she strategically took his two million dollars and flipped it, increasing it to six million dollars. Subsequently, with his consent, she invested his money by incorporating some businesses. One business she invested in was a waist trainer, Ka'oir Waist Erasers, which had a net worth of 10 million in 2017, which may be worth more today.

She said it looked like the worst time for him. He was looking at 20-years of incarceration, and she felt he needed her. Additionally, he needed guidance to help make him a better person. She proclaimed he had some issues with drugs, among other things. His walls were thick; she had to tell him to allow her to love him.

Additionally, she was not that kind of woman who was going to sit back and watch him damage his life. In her words, she broke it down to him like this: "I love you, and you need to come home to me." Also, she said, "I want you to be a better person for yourself so that you can be a better man for me." Nonetheless, with all the trouble he was going through, facing the maximum amount of time, Keyshia and Gucci prayed, and God answered all their prayers. She said to Gucci now your favor in return to God is to modify your life, and he did. After marriage, Keyshia says even with them having a household of two incomes, she does everything for him as a wife. She cooks, she cleans. She also said he fulfills his position as a husband, and the two are very happy. A question was posed to her because he has money; if he committed adultery, would it be easier to forgive him, opposed to a man with no money. She says she loves her husband, but no, she will not allow him to do anything to disrespect her because of who he is. However, she says because of the trust she has for him, that is not one of her worries. He does not have to worry about trusting her because he gave her 2 million dollars, and she did not spend a dime of it on herself. All she desired is for him to get out and be okay financially, mentally, and physically on top of her being a dedicated wife and mother. Kiesha also takes care of her relatives back home in Jamaica. There is much more to her story, as I said earlier.

Moreover, I just wanted to elaborate on the corresponding part, relevant to our topic: She was highly significant to his transformation financially and characteristically. Like was discussed in an earlier chapter, God will give you the wisdom and the resilience needed to be a helpmeet. On a Social Media Platform, Gucci Mane states in his words what she endured: "Everyone wants this, but what you all forget was she was with wild Gucci, on drugs Gucci, cheating Gucci, publicity with other women Gucci. I am the Gucci after therapy/rehabilitation. A street man groomed in his 30's after he's been at his lowest point. Point is this is a rider who knew what she signed up for! You ladies are with the next man after a couple of fights. I love my wife; she stayed down!" In an interview on the Dish Nation, a year into the marriage. Gucci Mane reflects on his relationship with his wife. Rickey Smiley asked him what does his wife get irritated with him about? He says his wife does not get annoyed with him; they do not have arguments. In his words: "Everything goes smooth they have such an adult, mature relationship."

"All married couples should examine themselves periodically and ask, what have we done with the resources God has given us? How are we handling His blessings? Are we spending our money wisely? Have we progressed over the past years? Are we moving in the right direction God wants us to go? Are we obeying His will? Is He pleased with our management? What does He want us to do next? These are important questions for growing in stewardship."

– Dr. Myles Monroe

Proverbs 31:20 (NIV)

"She opens her arms to the poor and extends her arms to the needy."

We have other prominent men like LeBron James Sr. from the Los Angeles Lakers that have made an impact on the basketball court as well as in society. Lebron, James acknowledges how his wife Savannah James as a very significant part of his success. He said He would not be the man he is today if it was not for his wife, which speaks to his character. He posted on one of the Social Media Platforms, "The only reason why I can do what I do at the highest level both on and off the floor is my best friend got my back regardless of the outcome. I am just the car; she is the engine! Appreciate you, Wonder Woman, aka Queen." In a recent interview from 2019, it was said; Savannah is a constant fixture in her husband's life. She has been by his side since their teenage years, but she is more than just the wife of a future Hall of Famer. As a child, Savannah James learned the importance of giving back to those in need from her parents. Her parents took in youngsters who were dealing with unfortunate circumstances. As an adult, she lends a helping hand to her husband's charity, the LeBron James Family Foundation. Giving back is essential to her. To add, she formulated a charity called "I Promise Make Over Campaign" What this campaign does is finds girls that do not have the funds to purchase their prom dresses, and they provide them with one. She and her husband are committed to philanthropy. Moreover, there is much more some do not know about this phenomenal virtuous woman. As Oprah Winfrey quoted, "all successful people have this in common servitude."

Proverbs 31:27 (NIV)

"She watches over the affairs of her household and does not eat the bread of idleness."

You never see her in the tabloids because she keeps her circle small. She has three close friends, and her parents that she confides in this is wise. The more people stay out of your business, the more successful your marriage will be. A virtuous woman does not invest her time gossiping (busybodies in other men's matters) because her time is spent taking care of her household. If you invest your time in someone else's business, that is an indication that something is lacking in your home. Taking care of a family is a full-time job that permits no time for foolishness or idle behavior. There is not enough time throughout the day, sometimes to take care of our responsibilities, let alone be in someone else's business. Besides, if we are not prioritizing our duties, meaning setting things in perspective as to its importance, it will affect our productivity. A housewife is a job in and of itself. If you have a job outside the house, that is a double responsibility. I know of no scripture reference that states that a woman's place is to clean up her house exclusively. It can be a shared responsibility. Those are decisions you and your spouse have to agree. However, if you are a stay-at-home wife and mom, it is your responsibility to manage the house. You should not be at home idle, talking to your girlfriends on the phone all day. Let me give you a few suggestions:

There are many ways to help your husband when he is a financial supporter. Many ways to let him know you appreciate him, affirmation, being attentive to his needs sexually, physically, and emotionally. Having your house clean, preparing tasty, nutritious meals, especially dinner, I am going to emphasize this "WHEN HE GETS HOME IT IS READY." So when he gets home, you will be done with all the household duties you can spend time with him. And if you have children with your children. Unless you guys decide otherwise (go out to eat.) Just as important, cover him in prayer from the chaos of the world and the wayward women.

Additionally, set the tone for your home, making it a haven and a place of serenity. Run his bathwater IJS, treat him how you would like to be treated. These are expressions of love; this is saying without speaking the word, I love you because love corresponds to an action. A relationship is solidified when the two are convinced they are loved, supported, and protected. He, as well as God, will honor your efforts.

Moreover, *another thing to what was said previously, it is very unattractive* to men when a woman is a gossiper. As a virtuous woman, he should be able to trust you with his life and his secrets. If he cannot confide in you, he will tell someone else. A wayward woman is always looking for an opportunity to catch you slipping.

Proverbs 20:19 (NIV)

"A gossip betrays a confidence; so, avoid a man (or woman) who talks too much."

Can a virtuous woman have a social life? Yes, she can! We do not have to be hermits; however, we do need to use DISCRETION, TEMPERANCE, and WISDOM! We need WISDOM for every functioning area of our lives. (finances, health, and wellness, marriage, family, household, friendships, job, etc.)

Nonetheless, everyone deserves a break and time for themselves, doing things they enjoy, with other people other than your spouse, if you all can agree. That is why it is imperative to communicate with your spouse. These are things you need to talk about BEFORE marriage as well as setting boundaries. What is respectful or reasonable and disrespectful or unreasonable to you in a relationship when it comes to outside relationships (same-sex and opposite-sex, single and married). You will be surprised what may be disrespectful or reasonable to one may not be rude or thoughtful to another. Especially when it comes to the opposite sex and single friend relationships. Allow me to say this, do not base your decisions about him around your insecurities or issues. That is why it is essential to be healed from all past hurts. Furthermore, know who you are, as we discussed earlier.

Nonetheless, we must have organization in our households. You can begin by establishing some reasonable goals for the day and complete them. Doing this first will help create DISCIPLINE and ORDER. When you start accomplishing your small (short-term) GOALS, then you can set some long-term goals. For your life mission, outline action steps and accompany them with the dates you desire to complete them for yourself as well as your family. These suggestions above can become your Action Plan!

Three More Attributes to Add to Managing your Household:

- Wisdom

- Discretion

- Goals

Proverbs 2:10-11 (NIV)

"For wisdom will enter your heart, and knowledge will be pleasant to your soul. Discretion will protect you, and understanding will guard you."

"One of the lessons that I grew up with was to always stay true to yourself and never let what somebody else says distract you from your goals. And so, when I hear about negative and false attacks. I really do not invest any energy in them, because I know who I am."

- Michelle Obama

Proverbs 31:17 (NIV)

"She set about her work vigorously; her arms are strong for her tasks"

If there is one place a woman is needed to be strong, it is the White House. To take on this position, with the opposition and scrutiny that comes with it, one needs strength. Consider Former First Lady, Michelle Obama. The whole world had their eyes on her being the wife of the President of the United States of America. As you all know, her husband was our nation's 44th President, Barack Obama. Before Michelle Obama was in her mother's womb, she was destined to be the first black, First Lady of our country. President Obama, along with Mrs. Obama, made history together. She was a great representation of Black Excellence with style and grace. Beholding all the qualities of a virtuous woman:

feminine, helpmeet, a wife, and mother with dignity and strength.

Proverbs 31:28 (NIV)

"Her children arise and call her blessed; her husband also and he praises her."

President Obama cries while talking about his wife, Michelle Obama. He says, for the last 25 years:

"You have not only been my wife and the mother of my children; you have been my best friend. You took on a role you did not ask for and made it your own with grace, grit, style, and humor. The new generation sets its heights higher because it has you as a role model. You have made me proud. You have made the country proud. "

President Obama, in one of his exit speeches from his presidency, said everything that he believes added value to him, their children, and the country. In his descriptive analogy, he spoke to her overall character. Be mindful of what you say and do in your household and public. Understand that you are a representation of God, first and foremost, your husband and your children. You may not be the First Lady of the United States of America, but you are the First Lady of YOUR household or maybe your church. Can your husband, children, and others speak well of you?

Proverbs 12:4 (NIV)

"A wife of noble character is her husband's crown, but a disgraceful wife is like decay in his bones."

Six Additional Attributes of a Wife with Noble Character

- Grace

- Grit (Courage and Strength of Character)

- Style

- Humor

- Role Model

- Dignity

"Let us *be very clear: Strong men – men who are truly role models. Do not need to put down women to make themselves feel powerful. People who are truly strong, lift others up. People who are truly powerful bring others together."* – Michelle Obama

CHAPTER 14

WOMEN OF DESTINY: GOD HAS A PLAN FOR YOU

Women of purpose are women of Destiny. When God destroyed the world in the time of Noah, the Bible says the heart of man was continuously evil. God repented that He ever created man. During this time, it's important to note, God's favor rested upon one man: Noah! God intended to create a new world using Noah and his family. The role of the wife (woman) was highly significant in this process of repopulation (regeneration). They needed their wives (THE WOMEN) whose names not mentioned in the Bible. Once again, the role of the woman was critical to God's plan, just as it was in the beginning with creation; (Genesis, Chapter 2) IT WAS THEIR DESTINY! With that said, without women, there wouldn't be any procreation in the earth! To be the most as one man quoted under-appreciated, unprotected, unattended, disregarded and disrespected people on the planet. God uses women to make an enormous contribution to the world. Women of old as well women of today! The greatest gift that ever graced this world is Jesus Christ…, who came from the womb of a woman, at that time she was a virgin. Mary, who was blessed and highly favored among all women; IT WAS HER DESTINY! (*See Matthew Chapter 1 and Luke Chapter 1*)

I declare in the Mighty Name of Jesus: "Arise women and take your rightful place. You are not a second-class citizen, a floor mat, a punching bag, or a sex object. You are POWERFUL, MIGHTY, STRONG, and SIGNIFICANT in the earth.!" Let me reiterate; God has given us the responsibility to teach the young, as was discussed earlier. We can't, however, accomplish that if we are not in our rightful place in mind, body, and spirit. God created everything to reproduce after its kind; you can only produce what you are. Let us make a conscious and continuous effort to continue the legacy and reproduce the Proverbs 31 Woman.

Additionally, continue to use our voice by sharing our testimonies to empower others; (sisters, neighbors, daughters, and friends) It may prevent someone from going through the same thing we went through. Let's also try to stop tearing down, degrading, and judging other women. Make a concerted effort to use our energy to lift one another. When you see a sister fall, help boost her back up. You see her going down the wrong road, help get her back on track. Let's demolish the mythical saying that women can't get along, yes, we can, by utilizing respect and establishing boundaries. I'm learning if you don't have anything good to say, don't say anything at all. Jesus says in John 7:24; stop judging by mere appearances and make a right judgment. It's hard to make the right judgment when you don't know a person's story. We can make assumptions, but are our assumptions TRUE? We must stand on truth, follow truth, and speak the truth.

Ephesians 4:29 (NIV)

"Do not let any unwholesome talk come out of your mouths, but only what is helpful for building others up according to their needs, that it may benefit those who listen."

We have one enemy, and his name is Satan. Let us expeditiously use our God-given authority against him, and not each other. By taking back our voice, dominion, positions, household, husband, children, relationships, and families! Some women don't know how powerful they are to the Body of Christ and within society. Partly because of error, what you have, or have not been taught correctly.

Consequently, because we haven't been on our post. The devil has been wreaking havoc over this nation and the Body of Christ. One day a thought came to mind, where are the Church Mothers? The church mothers were those that sat on the front row, adorned in their white, and who we depended on to labor in prayer with us and give wise counsel. We rarely see them in the church building anymore because the elderly, seasoned mothers have either passed away, and the position has grown extinct within the modern-day church. However, it's still very much needed today. God has anointed women to the area of prayer; when it is absent, we see the turmoil we are experiencing in the world today. Some have allowed the position (of the church mother) to pass away. How did it move away? BECAUSE IT WASN'T PASSED ON! A famous quote by Dr. Maya Angelo: "When you learn teach. When you get give"

Jeremiah 9:17-21 (NIV)

"This is what the Lord Almighty says: Consider now! Call for the wailing women to come; send for the most skillful of them. Let them come quickly and wail over us till our eyes overflow with tears and water streams from our eyelids. The sound of waling is heard from Zion: How ruined we are! How great is our shame! We must leave our land because our houses are in ruins. NOW, O women, hear the word of the Lord; open your ears to the words of his mouth. Teach your daughters how to wail; teach one another a lament. Death has climbed in through our windows and has entered our fortresses..."

There is a particular sound (cry) that a mother makes when her children are in distress. That holds with God as well. That sound (wailing) gets God's attention; God responded to the children of Israel when they cried out for deliverance from the hands of Pharaoh in Egypt. Not only did He hear their cry, He saw their misery, and He sent a deliverer (Moses). Recognize and submit to your deliverers. Your deliverers are those persons God has sent to help and guide you out of situations. There are nations of people being held captive and awaiting the prayers of the righteous to be set free. Prayer is the most potent weaponry that God has given us along with Faith and Love.

Ephesians 6:16 (KJV)

"Above all, taking the shield of faith, wherewithal ye shall be able to quench all the fiery darts of the wicked."

Ephesians 6:18 (KJV)

"Praying always with all prayer and supplication in the Spirit, and watching thereunto with all perseverance and supplication for all saints;"

1 Peter 4:8 (NIV)

"Above all, love each other deeply, because love covers over a multitude of sins."

Women of the 21-century, we must use our weapons. We are the women of change, faith, and DESTINY! God has always used women and put them in powerful positions in ministry, business, politics, social climate, and motherhood; to make a difference and as modern-day change agents within society and our households. The past women of DESTINY, as well as the future women of DESTINY, had to overcome monumental challenges, obstacles, and great adversities to achieve their goals.

I'll share another experience:

One day I was in the basement at my Hair Salon, and my ex-husband's father came to visit. We had cameras with audio sound located in various parts of the salon. One was downstairs where I was, and there was one at the front door. I overheard my ex-father-in-law telling my ex-husband not to trust women, subtly referring to me. He used Eve as an example. He said, you see what happened to Adam. Women have been the downfall of man ever since. It was Eve's fault what happened in the garden. In actuality, his father was also saying, don't trust the woman from wents you came. Or any female for that matter. I found what he was saying very offensive; one because he was referring to me. Two, through his rhetoric, he was planting a negative seed in my ex-husband's mind, which would negatively affect my marriage. What he was teaching him was not to have confidence in me. Not by my inconsistent behavior, but by gender alone! If he didn't have confidence in me from the start, how was I supposed to help him? However, I can admit I was ignorant about the two types of women until God revealed it to me. I was in the category of a wayward woman before I believed and allowed the Holy Spirit to transform me. Being the right person wasn't good enough; I needed to be converted from the inside. Consequently, the judgement of women came by one woman's actions (Eve.) She wasn't just any old ordinary woman, of course. She was the very first woman created in God's image. She set the standard for every woman reproduced after her (sinners.) She is the mother of us all, every living thing. It's sad to say that this is not only a stain concerning the woman because of Eve. Also, this stigma is passing down from generation to generation. Unfortunately, this wasn't something that my ex's father-in-law just so happened to conjure. Apostle Paul also taught the very same thing to Timothy.

1 Timothy 2:12-12 (NIV)

"I do not permit a woman to teach or to have authority over a man; she must be silent. For Adam was formed first, then Eve. And Adam was not the one deceived; it was the woman who was deceived and became a sinner."

That's why we have to divide the Word of God rightly. Apostle Paul uses the word: "I" (someone aware of possessing a personal individuality), which denotes this is his own opinion. His father and Paul were partially wrong because it wasn't her fault alone; both of them were at fault and became sinners. Yes, there is no argument; it was because Adam listened to the woman these things transpired. (See Genesis 3:17.) However, my ex's Father-in-law and Paul left out one truth: JESUS! When Jesus came through the womb of Mary, salvation came, the curse and the stigma broke for the believer. His blood removed the stain that beset us. The Bible says God told Joseph to call Him Jesus, because He will save His people from sin (See Matthew 1:21) Regardless of what man may think about us, not all women because of Jesus fit in the same category (wayward). What sets us apart is not the clothes we wear, the way we wear our hair (natural or straight), our walk, and talk. What sets us apart, no matter what cultural background we come from, our belief and faith in Jesus. His Godly values, and morals, the Godly standard of holiness. Holiness in the Greek translation is derived from the word: hagiasmos (hag-ee-as-mos), which means sanctification (the process of advancing in holiness); use of the believer being progressively transformed by the Lord into His likeness (similarity of nature).

Romans 8:29 (NIV)

"For those God foreknew he also predestined to be conformed to the likeness of His Son, that He might be the firstborn among many brothers."

I pray by now; you can answer these questions with no reservation.

"Who are you? Whose are you? Why are you here? Where am I from? What can I do? And where am I going, what is my destination? Are you a fighter or a quitter? Are you victorious or a victim? What type of woman are you? What's your purpose?" More importantly, are you willing to do whatever is necessary to reach your destiny? Ruth did not know her future; however, it was already divinely planned for her by God. Your Ruth experience is already scheduled for you; by God, just continue to believe in the process. For example, a beautiful Rose, before it reaches its full potential (manifestation) and values it has to go through all the necessary procedures to get there, seed, time, and harvest.

In conclusion, if no one else thinks highly of you in this lifetime, remember God does! He expresses how He feels about you in His Word: (Proverbs 3:13-15). I pray that you will accept His validation and vision of you. And protect your virtue. If it weren't for God (Jesus), I wouldn't be here today, in my right mind. I believe that if I had continued one more day without Him, my past would have taken me out. Words cannot express how grateful l am. To inherit the full benefits and promises of God and His Word, we must receive Jesus Christ as our Lord and Savior. If you are one that has not received Him, it's a simple process. All you have to do is believe in Jesus and repent of your sins. You will then begin your new journey in this love relationship. Just open up your heart and allow Him to come in and fill you with His precious gift of the Holy Spirit. Say these words:

"Father, forgive me of my sins, I (name) confess with my heart and believe in my heart that God raised Jesus from the dead."

Romans 10:9 (NIV)

"That if you confess with your mouth, 'Jesus Christ is Lord' and believe in your heart that God raised Jesus from the dead, you will be saved."

Acts 2:38 (NIV)

"Peter replied, Repent and be baptized, every one of you, in the name of Jesus Christ so that your sins may be forgiven. And you will receive the gift f the Holy Spirit."

If you received the Lord Jesus Christ as your Lord and Savior, welcome to the Family of God! I am not going to tell you a lie and say that it's going to be easy. These things come with the territory: Persecution, Affliction, and Trouble, why? Because we have a common adversary. However, I will tell you that it is better to go through them (trials) with Him (Jesus) than without Him! He made a solemn promise to deliver us from them all. Look to Him the author and the finisher of our Faith (See: Hebrews 12:2)

Love and Peace be with you always, thanks for your listening ear. Remember, don't settle for anything less than the best; you are worth it! **YOU ARE A WOMEN OF PURPOSE AND DESTINY!**

ABOUT THE AUTHOR

Latricia Taylor is an emerging author born in Atlanta, Georgia, raised in Flint, MI, in a single-parent home. For the majority of her life, she didn't know who she was. It wasn't until Latricia established a relationship with God; Latricia discovered her self-worth and identity. She is a survivor of domestic violence, not once, twice but three times. Through her experience, God gave her a voice and a testimony to aid other women in the faith.